Biblical Nuggets

HAPPY BIRTHDAY.

YOUR BEAUTIFUL.

LOVE,

JOHN

by John Klein
with Michael Christopher

1

Biblical Nuggets

Published by Lost in Translation
© 2015 by John Klein with Michael Christopher

ISBN-10: 151506624x
ISBN-13: 978-1515066248

Cover design by Katie Klein
email: katie@katiekleinsmm.com
URL: katiekleinsmm.com

Lost in Translation
PO Box 8224
Bend, OR 97708
www.lostintranslation.org

Introduction

During the course of our biblical studies over the last twenty-five years we've discovered several interesting insights into the Hebrew Scriptures. For example, probably very little of what we've included in this publication would have seen the light of day if we hadn't learned a long time ago to approach everything from an Hebraic perspective. No matter how many times we translate it into other languages the Bible is still an Hebraic book, which introduces several important considerations.

Undoubtedly the most important would be the Hebraic approach to writing history, recording recommendations, and even laying out God's law. The same basic approach shows up over and over, beginning in Genesis and ending in Revelation. At the same time it's quite simple, involving just two basic things. First, the ancient Hebrews usually began each written series of observations with a short summary that essentially spelled out what was coming next, perhaps to give the reader a "feel" for what the writer wanted to say. This would then be followed by as many details, both broad-based and intricate, as the author felt necessary to convey his full intent.

The first and possibly the clearest example of this unique approach occurs in the first few chapters of Genesis. In these passages God Himself provides an overall summary of the original "Days of Creation," followed by a series of details that essentially fill in the blanks by amplifying and clarifying some of the specifics that came before.

But again . . . this is only one example of how the Bible itself, in its overall approach and its specific language, conveys the "full story" and provides the reader with the understanding he or she needs to comprehend God's nature, His purposes, and His hopes for the salvation of mankind.

So . . . given all that, we hope that the following short, individual insights into the organization, the specific language itself, the history it reveals, and many other considerations will help you more fully understand and more tenderly treasure the Bible yourself.

Essentially, we have tried to highlight some of the "Aha!" moments that we've had in our own studies of the Scriptures. We've grouped them into seven different categories:

> Science and the Bible
> End Times
> Personal Relationships with God
> From an Hebraic Perspective
> Biblical History
> Hebrew Language and Pictographs
> Biblical Feasts

You will find these individual sections more fully introduced in the Table of Contents, so that when you do your own research you'll be able to more quickly find what interests you the most.

Table of Contents

1 — Personal Relationships with God

Salvation Has a Signature

As you make bigger commitments in your own life, to serve God and to war against everything that causes chaos in your own soul, God draws you closer to Himself. And, as he draws you closer He gives you greater responsibility and authority. Thus the whole range of our potential relationship to God is pictured in the menorah (i.e., the seven-lamp Hebrew lamp stand) by the proximity of the players to the Groom, who is positioned in the middle, often the taller lamp known as the "Shamash."

For example, both Adam and Noah were asked to serve God. When they responded He gave them greater responsibility and authority. On the other hand, God gave David a lot more of practically everything — he was the apple of God's eye and was in an extremely close relationship with God. David got tremendous responsibility and ever-increasing authority all the way through his life.

Many people today want to start off being the Bride. But covenant with God doesn't begin anywhere near there; it starts with being a servant. Likewise, some people think that once you get your ticket to heaven, via "salvation," you're free to do whatever you want. This also is not true, and anyone who teaches such a philosophy has little or no understanding of what the Scriptures actually say.

On the contrary, James said, "I will show you my faith by my works" (James 2:18). We need to operate by the same standard. Faith is not just a warm fuzzy feeling — it's an active force that essentially "proves" the salvation that lies within you, which constantly rises to the surface.

Or doesn't.

Has Torah Really Been Abolished?

If you want to be the Bride of Yeshua (i.e., Christ Himself) you should be about doing the will of the Father and not forgetting what you look like. James speaks about this very issue:

> [21]Therefore, get rid of all moral filth and the evil that is so prevalent and humbly accept the word planted in you, which can save you. [22]Do not merely listen to the word, and so deceive yourselves. Do what it says. [23]Anyone who listens to the word but does not do what it says is like a man who looks at his face in a mirror [24]and, after looking at himself, goes away and immediately forgets what he looks like. [25]But the man who looks intently into the perfect law that gives freedom, and continues to do this, not forgetting what he has heard, but doing it – he will be blessed in what he does. (James 1:21–25, NIV)

The Hebrew term for *word* in the passage above is *Torah*. This passage suggests that we should integrate Torah into our very soul so it becomes the standard that governs our every action. Our behavior, our works, and our thoughts should all mirror holiness. Yeshua said that we should look like Him. He also said in John 1:1 that He was *the Word,* which is Torah. And John was referring to the Old Testament at this point because the New Testament did not yet exist.

In our passage above, James talks about procuring freedom by obeying the perfect law. Again, this phrase is a clear reference to the Torah, because the Torah is perfect and it constitutes the principles for holy living that we should incorporate into our lives just as Yeshua did. In so doing we clearly identify who we are attempting to model our lives by, and that is Yeshua. John makes the same reference to Yeshua in his first chapter, when he calls the Messiah the "Word," again referring to Torah.

Standing Up for Good

Satan is perfectly happy with believers who do nothing, stand for nothing, and say nothing in the face of evil. As the well-known quote by Edmund Burke says, "All that is necessary for the triumph of evil is for good men to do nothing."

Do our lives stand for something when we're faced with the temptations of the Adversary? Do we melt and find excuses? Or, are we confused whenever we're confronted with his deceptions? His temptations bring only bondage but they never look like that when they're first offered. Meanwhile, God knows every single plan Satan can dredge up and is never caught off guard. He anticipates every one of Satan's attempts at revenge and provides protection.

One of the many reasons why our nation is in the condition it is in today is because the believers have not stood up and opposed very clear deviations from the truth. Our morals have collapsed, and the principles on which our founding fathers built the constitution are ignored and reinterpreted by non-believing "authorities." All the while, the Church stands silently by. Take a quick look at the verse below.

> If my people, who are called by my name, will humble themselves and pray and seek my face and turn from their wicked ways, then I will hear from heaven, and I will forgive their sin and will heal their land. (2 Chronicles 7:14, NIV)

Who is God talking to here? He's talking to His people, not non-believers. And he says that if *His* people seek *His* face, He will hear them, forgive their sins, and heal their land. Judgment falls not because nonbelievers are filling the land with sin; it happens because believers are not listening to God and obeying Him.

The Apple of His Eye

In Proverbs 7:2, God indicates that He wants us to cherish His teachings as "the apple of your [our] eye." Also, in Psalm 17:8 and Zechariah 2:8, He used very intimate language to describe the relationship that He wants to have with His people, by calling them "the apple of His [my] eye."

To further describe the value and place of honor that God gives to man, especially those who obey Him, He uses the word *Yeshurun* four times in the Old Testament to describe His people. These references are included below. This word is a tender, loving reference to the people who are truly His.

Sometimes He even uses this description in the midst of their gross misbehavior. This communicates the fact that even in spite of our sin and disobedience to His ways, God is still able to see us as He hopes we will become. It is our choice to actually be Yeshurun. This word, literally, means "to be straight or upright in all that we do." The word also can be defined as "being level," as in living your life in a way that respects God and your fellow man.

> Jeshurun grew fat and kicked;
>   filled with food, they became heavy and sleek.
> They abandoned the God who made them
>   and rejected the Rock their Savior.
> (Deuteronomy 32:15, NIV)

> He was king over Jeshurun
> when the leaders of the people assembled,
> along with the tribes of Israel.
> (Deuteronomy 33:5, NIV)

> "There is no one like the God of Jeshurun,
>   who rides across the heavens to help you
>   and on the clouds in his majesty.
> (Deuteronomy 33:26, NIV)

God has called all believers to follow His principles for holy living. What do all believers do upon becoming saved? They repent and ask for forgiveness. Why is repenting part of salvation if there is no law? What are they repenting for? If there is no law, can sin even exist? If there is no law, what do we need to be saved from?

We are being saved from the very violations of the same law that God gave Moses on Mount Zion in the Old Testament. That law was applicable then and we're still being saved from violations of the same law today. Jesus did not come to abolish the law. He came to abolish the penalty for violating the law, thereby making us righteous.

Are We Righteous or Holy – or Both?
Those who propose that we cannot become holy through the blood of Yeshua are technically correct. This is true especially if they believe that by accepting the blood

13

sacrifice of Yeshua as remediation for their sins they attain righteousness, not holiness.

Unfortunately, many who assert the above also make no distinction between (1) *righteousness* – which is what we attain through salvation and faith – and (2) *holiness*, which is what we can attain by making an active choice to do so. Righteousness is a *result of salvation through faith*, whereas holiness results from our choice to *redefine the essence of ourselves.*

Here's how James, Yeshua's own brother, put it:

> [14]What use is it, my brethren, if someone says he has faith but he has no works? Can that faith save him? [15]If a brother or sister is without clothing and in need of daily food, [16]and one of you says to them, "Go in peace, be warmed and be filled," and yet you do not give them what is necessary for their body, what use is that? [17]Even so faith, if it has no works, is dead, being by itself. (James 2:14–17)

In other words, James never claimed that works can substitute or "stand in" for faith. We cannot have a saving relationship with the Lord [i.e., we cannot become righteous] by doing good deeds and relying on those. Since sin first entered our world God has made it very clear that salvation, meaning *our ability to have a meaningful relationship with God and eventually to spend eternity in His presence*, requires (1) confession of our sins and (2) acceptance of His pardon for those sins, made possible by the sacrifice of His Son.

However, once we have confessed and accepted forgiveness, through faith in God's willingness to forgive

us, as we build a "working relationship" with Him He
begins to "link up" with us spiritually so that we desire,
more and more, to be as much like Him as possible. At
that point we begin to show love, compassion, and a
desire to help others exactly as He shows those things to
us.

And that is the essence of holiness. In other words, only
as we begin to yearn for and eventually achieve holiness
will our good works have any lasting, eternal value.

So . . . does any of the above suggest that we can live our
lives any way we want? Have the actual words of God,
defining what holiness is, been done away with?
Remember, these ideals are the very principles that
define God's own holiness. If the principles for holy
living explained in the Old Testament really have been
abolished, would that also abolish the holiness of God?

Covenant Means Restoration
God is in the process of restoring man back to what he
was before the fall in the Garden of Eden. Man's body,
soul, and spirit fell from a perfect 777 to a 666 (the
number of man, Revelation 13:18).

In this process of restoration, man's spirit is restored
first. This was made possible when Yeshua died on the
cross. At that moment the restoration of the spirit
became available for anyone who wanted to accept God's
free gift and enter into relationship with Him. Over the
past 2,000 years, many have accepted that relationship
and have been restored to a position of 766.

Those who died before Yeshua's death on the Cross, but

believed in the Creator God, were also restored to a position of 7-6-6 at Yeshua's resurrection. They were transferred from the grave into the presence of God at that same moment in time (I Peter 3:19).

Man's soul is being mended and restored through covenant. When man dies or Yeshua returns, man is restored to a 776. The restoration of the body occurs last "in the twinkling of an eye" and will once again render man as a 777, the same as he was before the fall. We will be given new bodies that cannot suffer death. This will occur starting at the last trumpet during the Second Coming and will be completed at the Great White Throne Judgment that comes at the end of the thousand-year reign.

In addition to the above, I Corinthians 15 adds more information about this evolution. It seems that man began with a spirit, mind, and body that were a bit different than the final state represented by 777 above. Paul implies that the first Adam was created mortal, but the second Adam, and the body given to all those who are believers in God, will be immortal.

Restoration is a process, and it all involves covenant and commitment to being obedient to God. We have much to do, and much to look forward to.

How to Complement God's Plan

God's plan was first revealed to mankind almost from the start of our existence. Throughout the ages, as revealed in the biblical text, God gave us additional details in regard to His intentions for His creation and for us. If you have read our other books, especially *Lost in*

Translation: Rediscovering the Hebrew Roots of Our Faith, you are aware of the greatest of all gifts given to mankind — restored relationship with God. In the Bible He called this relationship "covenant."

We also learned that there are four relationships to be had through covenant: service, friendship, manager, and bridal. These were given to mankind and represented our part in the restoration process. God has asked us to step into these relationships in a logical sequence, with each one requiring additional responsibilities.

God's plan is complemented when we conform our lives to His principles. If you haven't read the first book in the *Lost in Translation* trilogy, this might be a good time to do so. It will greatly enhance your insight into what you can do to fulfill His plans for you.

How God Wishes to Be Approached

At both the Temple in Jerusalem and the tabernacle in the wilderness, the throat of each sacrificial animal would be cut before the animal would be placed on the bronze altar in the outer court of the Tabernacle grounds. This offering was called *korban* in Hebrew. The root word that korban comes from is *kerabah*. Its primary meaning is "to approach or draw near."

In other words, within the word for sacrifice God embedded His primary message to mankind: As you humble yourself by recognizing your shortfalls you may draw near to Me. This is why God tells the Israelites that He hates their sacrifices.

> Alas, you who are longing for the day of the LORD,
> For what purpose *will* the day of the LORD *be* to you?

17

It *will be* darkness and not light;
¹⁹ As when a man flees from a lion
And a bear meets him,
Or goes home, leans his hand against the wall
And a snake bites him.
²⁰ *Will* not the day of the L<small>ORD</small> *be* darkness instead of light,
Even gloom with no brightness in it?

²¹ "I hate, I reject your festivals,
Nor do I delight in your solemn assemblies.
²² "Even though you offer up to Me burnt offerings and your
grain offerings, I will not accept *them*;
And I will not *even* look at the peace offerings of your
fatlings. ²³ "Take away from Me the noise of your songs;
I will not even listen to the sound of your harps.
²⁴ "But let justice roll down like waters
And righteousness like an ever-flowing stream.
(Amos 5:18–24)

He is not rescinding His commands with respect to the offering of sacrifices. Rather, God is telling us that offering up the symbol without real repentance is just the empty practice of religion rather than its true, meaningful substance. The Hebrew word for religion is *dot*. The pictographic message embedded within the letter symbols communicates to us what true religion is. The pictographic understanding of *dalet/tav* tells us that our religious practices should be our pathway to the sign of the covenant. If they do not reward us with greater intimacy with our Creator we are defeating their purpose.

That is why God said:

"Pure and undefiled religion in the sight of *our* God and Father is this: to visit orphans and widows in their distress, *and* to keep oneself unstained by the world" (James 1:27).

18

The sacrifice of animals was to remind the Israelites of the Son who would come as a perfect Lamb and would lay down his life willingly, as an offering to pay the price for sin. This had been taught through many passages in Torah, given to the Israelites on Mt. Sinai. As man recalls the price that was paid for his sin, God's hope is that we will approach Him humbly, ask for His forgiveness, and repent.

The Hebrew word *dot*, which conveys the idea of religion, has another meaning. This word also refers to the laws that were the foundation of Torah, which are described there as principles for holy living. So, embedded within the word religion we find the principles and the laws that God wants us to follow. In addition, these principles explain how to properly draw near to him as well.

This then implies that without a proper understanding of the laws of God it's impossible to draw near to Him.

Rebirth and Our True Nature

The Hebrew word for repent is *shuv*, spelled *shen/vav/vet*. Its primary meaning is "to turn about, to return." The idea is that, when one sins, true repentance is not just asking for forgiveness but also includes turning away from our sinful ways and returning to our true nature.

That true nature derives from our rebirth as sons and daughters of God, for at that moment we are no longer sons of man, characterized by the sinful nature we acquired from the first Adam. We now carry the nature of our new Father, which is righteousness. And, we are now called to a new walk, one of holiness. A walk of holiness is the way a righteous son or daughter acts and thinks.

> For I am the LORD who brought you up from the land of
> Egypt to be your God; thus you shall be holy, for I am holy.'"
> (Leviticus 11:45)
> "Speak to all the congregation of the sons of Israel and say to
> them, 'You shall be holy, for I the LORD your God am holy."
> (Leviticus 19:2)
>
> Because it is written, "YOU SHALL BE HOLY, FOR I AM HOLY."
> (1 Peter 1:16)

God wants us to double our efforts to draw close to Him
by trying to understand His nature. He wants us to obey
Him first, then to be His friend, then to be His sons and
daughters, and ultimately to be His bride.

God's final goal is revealed by the constellation known as
Capricorn (see *Anatomy of the Heavens*, listed in the
Recommended Reading section -at the end of this text,
for more information). As a man and a women become
one when they become married, we become one with our
Creator through the covenants of service, friendship,
inheritance, and then finally marriage. The fish and the
goat in Capricorn, depicted by an image that is part fish
and part goat, exemplify the concept of becoming one. As
they are pictured in the sky, so they exemplify God's goal
for mankind, which is for mankind to become one with
Him.

The goat represents the Son of God, and the fish
represents mankind. In Scripture, fish are sometimes
used metaphorically to represent people, or Israel.

> And He said to them, "Follow Me, and I will make you
> fishers of men." (Matthew. 4:19)

"Again, the kingdom of heaven is like a dragnet cast into the sea, and gathering *fish* of every kind; 48 and when it was filled, they drew it up on the beach; and they sat down and gathered the good *fish* into containers, but the bad they threw away. (Matthew 13:47–48)

'As the LORD lives, who brought up the sons of Israel from the land of the north and from all the countries where He had banished them.' For I will restore them to their own land which I gave to their fathers. 16"Behold, I am going to send for many fishermen," declares the LORD, "and they will fish for them; and afterwards I will send for many hunters, and they will hunt them from every mountain and every hill and from the clefts of the rocks. (Jeremiah 16:15–16)

It will come about that every living creature which swarms in every place where the river goes, will live. And there will be very many fish, for these waters go there and *the others* become fresh; so everything will live where the river goes. (Ezekiel 47:9)

In Hebrew the sign for life is the fish, because of its ability to make quick, vibrant movements as it darts through the water. God's desire is to reunite and restore the broken relationship between us and Himself. Someday He will accomplish His goal and place His bride on a throne at His side, from which they will rule and reign together over creation.

2 — Science and the Bible

Should Doctors Read the Bible?
Several centuries ago it was a common medical practice to "bleed" people who were suffering from various types of ailments. As with so many other false scientific concepts that have existed over the last thousand years, if the same people had read their Bibles they would have realized that the very last thing you want to do to a person — especially a sick one — is to "bleed them out."

Today we know of many reasons why this was a very deleterious medical practice. But even without today's knowledge, God embedded in His Word the knowledge and instruction that could have saved a lot of lives. If only we would be students of the Bible.

What Does Science Have to Do with It?
Some people believe that the bible stands apart from the scientific world. Many times these same people — especially those who simply do not wish to believe in a creator God because of what they fear He might require of them — even suggest that the Bible disagrees with scientific facts.

Actually, many scientific principles were contained first within the biblical text and were validated much later by scientific discoveries, as man's awareness and understanding of his surroundings gradually developed over the centuries. These biblical-scientific principles include revolutionary ideas, (1) such as the earth is not flat but is in fact a sphere; (2) that the earth orbits around the sun and not the other way around; (2) that the universe had a definite beginning and has not always existed. (4) that bleeding sick people would not result in the restoration of health but would actually hinder the healing process.

All these — and many more — are supported by the words in the Bible, and are further verified by scientific thinking today.

The modern scientific community is also aware that four forces manage and control all matter. Whether we consider the movements of planets, the forces involved with the weather on planet earth, or the structure and workings of the atom, these four forces influence all of their interactions. They include gravity, electromagnetism, the lesser atomic, and the greater atomic forces.

We have also learned that God has given mankind four forces with which to influence his surroundings and complete the work given to him by God through covenant. What
God is saying is . . .

1) If you want to be effective in My kingdom, serve others.

2) Making friends is a great way to be influential.

3) Managing other people's concerns and assets well will have great rewards.

4) The marriage relationship is the most intimate but also the most powerful if you want to influence the

world around you.

So . . . the next time you want to accomplish something, start by serving others.

Three "isms" in God's Creation

Numerous triads of foundational supports can be found in God's creation. For example, on the first day God created three things – time, space, and matter, which are often referred to as the "time-space-matter continuum." Each one of these can then be best understood by recognizing that it is defined by three separate "aspects" or parts:

1) Space is defined by height, width, and depth.

2) Time is defined by past, present, and future.

3) Matter is defined by the three forms in which it occurs — liquid, gas, and solid.

God is the *fourth* "force" that binds all the above together. It's interesting that He also created four elementary forces that hold everything together on a physical level, on both the smallest and the largest playing fields — (1) gravity, (2) electro-magnetic attraction, and (3) the greater atomic force, which keeps the nucleus of atoms together, and (4) the lesser atomic force, which keeps the atoms of creation in an orderly state.

These four forces are well known to modern science. However, what creates these forces is, by-and-large, not known at all. We do not know how one object can attract another. What is the actual origin of the force that draws the moon to the earth? What is the actual force that keeps the electrons spinning around the protons and neutrons in the atom, and how does that force accomplish that feat? By and large, science can only provide guesses and conjectures.

I'm sure that there are answers, and the Bible actually does refer to those answers. It says:

> And He is the radiance of His glory and the exact representation of His nature, and upholds all things by the word of His power. When He had made purification of sins, He sat down at the right hand of the Majesty on high. (Hebrews 1:3)

Is it possible that the very powers and forces that hold our earth and universe together actually come from the hands of God?

Olfactory Excellence

The formula for the ancient incense that God provided His priests to use in His temple — and which He required them to guard carefully — has truly amazing properties that function on at least two major levels at once. First, given the large numbers of animals that were slaughtered as offerings every day, it would be perfectly logical to expect to encounter some horrendous smells. Even modern meatpacking plants, using modern refrigeration, advanced ventilation systems, and featuring the very best in additional odor-control procedures, do not very often provide pleasant olfactory experiences. But when the incense produced by the God-given formula is burned it has the amazing ability to almost completely "knock down" and mask any unpleasant smells that might otherwise rule the daily air.

More amazing still, all the flies and other insects that would normally be attracted in overwhelming numbers were completely held at bay. Those flies don't hunt at all! The result is another of God's magnificent "hedges of protection" that sheltered His people when they did what He prescribed in the way that He prescribed it. In other words, the incense doubled as God's fumigation system.

What Does Color Have to Do with It?
Have you ever wondered what causes things to be certain colors? Mankind and the creation that surrounds him do not give off colors that originate within themselves. They have only the capacity to absorb and reflect light, which usually comes from the sun. They absorb most of the color spectrum in white light and reflect just a small portion of certain parts of the color spectrum.

That reflected light is what our eyes pick up. In other words, things that are blue are blue only because they reflect blue light while absorbing the other colors of the light spectrum.

Because God dwells in His people we should act as conduits for His light, not reflectors. Reflectors only pretend to be sources of light, but God's people should know that their thoughts and actions can be conduits of His light, to the world, revealing Truth. Truth should be the focus for His people. They should not think that they are the light's origins but should humbly recognize the true source.

The Physics of Light and Color

God is light (1 John 1:5) and is clothed in light (Psalm 104:2). His goal is to restore man back to the fullness of white light, to make us as mature in Him as we are willing to be.

The purpose of covenant is restoration of relationship with our Creator. The three primary types of covenant – blood, salt, and sandal – correspond to what some claim are the three primary colors (red, yellow, and blue). God initiates these covenants.

What some claim are the secondary colors (orange, green, and purple) show man's positive response to God's offer of covenant. The ultimate is the covenant of marriage, which is a combination of the three primary types and should correspond to the color white. However, physics teaches us that the three primary colors do not combine to give white light as we would expect. Why is this?

White light is composed of all colors, but red, green, and blue are the minimum that can combine to give white light. In fact, with light, green is said to be a primary color, not yellow. Why is green a secondary color in pigment but a primary color in light?

This is true for the same reason that the Son lowered Himself to a state below even that of the angels (Hebrews 2:9), yet is still the Sovereign of the Universe. The three primary colors of light represent God and the order of the work that is done for the process of restoration. As Ephesians 2:18 explains, the Spirit must draw you to the Son so that you can receive from the Father.

Red   = the Spirit

Green = the Son

Blue   = the Father

The Son is green instead of yellow because He is a combination of the divine and the earthly. The second part of the Godhead came to earth as both God and man. He became a "secondary color" in terms of earthly pigment out of His great love for us, but will always be a primary color in terms of light.

A Truly Unique Rainbow

We believe that, prior to Noah's time, the earth was watered by springs rather than by storm systems. After the great Flood, Noah saw a rainbow, given to him as a sign that God would never again destroy the earth with a flood. The following text from Genesis 9 strongly implies that this was the first rainbow Noah had ever seen:

> "I set my bow in the cloud, and it shall be for a sign of a covenant between Me and the earth. [14]It shall come about, when I bring a cloud over the earth, that the bow will be seen in the cloud, [15]and I will remember My covenant, which is between Me and you and every living creature of all flesh; and never again shall the water become a flood to destroy all flesh. [16]When the bow is in the cloud, then I will look upon it, to remember the everlasting covenant between God and every living creature of all flesh that is on the earth." [17]And God said to Noah, "This is the sign of the covenant which I have established between Me and all flesh that is on the earth." (Genesis 9:13–17)

The words God spoke to Noah also suggest that it had never significantly rained before. Rainbows are caused by the refraction of light from the sun as it interacts with the water in raindrops. Surely this would have happened before had rain been a common phenomenon before the Flood began.

Where Does Astrology Fit into the REAL Picture?

In ancient civilizations, each section of thirty degrees of the Earth's orbit around the sun represented the distance the moon appeared to move through the stars and the twelve constellations each month, from our earthly perspective. Modern astrologers still believe that these thirty-degree sections represent the amount of time that the moon still spends in each section, which the early astrologers called "houses."

Unfortunately, these houses, which are known to astrologers by the names of the twelve constellations (and are also called the "signs of the zodiac"), are all assigned thirty degrees of orbital travel even though the amounts of such travel involved in each one actually vary greatly. Therefore the twelve constellations occupy different
sized portions of the complete circle, which highlights a huge logical fallacy with respect to the rigid thirty-day time frame each "sign of the zodiac" is given.

How can the claimed relationships between the zodiacal "signs" of our birth be considered significant when millions of us have not been born during what might appear (from our perspective) to be the moon's travel through a particular zodiac, but could be keyed to that so-called travel through one of the zodiacs traversed either before or after the one during which we were supposedly born?

The North Pole Has Not Always Been Oriented Toward Polaris

Four to five thousand years ago, Thuban, one of the stars in the constellation Draco, was the pole star. Draco, the dragon, has always been a constellation that represented Satan. The pole star is the North Star, which all the constellations and stars revolve around from our earthly perspective.

This emulates Satan's own longstanding desire. He very much wants mankind to focus and spin around him. Satan wants to be at the center of God's creation, being worshiped by all and having the authority to rule over everything.

Over time, the center that the constellations revolve around has migrated due to the procession of the stars away from Draco. Instead of the stars of Draco being used for navigation, as the ancients did, the North Star is now Polaris. The "Guiding Star," Polaris, has taken the place of the dragon! The bible speaks about god being the guiding start that should light our way, and He should be the center of our lives!

What light do you use for navigation in your life?

Is It a System or Just One Star?

Polaris is not a single star but rather a star system. It includes a bright, super-giant star, which is the one we can see clearly with our naked eyes. But orbiting very closely are two additional stars. These two are much smaller in size and are virtually invisible to anyone not using a telescope. Even then, they are seen traveling around this super giant at a very close range. What does

31

all of this mean?

These stars may be suggesting that there is only one God, as His Word suggests.

> "I am the LORD, and there is no other; Besides Me there is no God.
> I will gird you, though you have not known Me. (Isaiah 45:5)
>
> The scribe said to Him, "Right, Teacher; You have truly stated that HE IS ONE, AND THERE IS NO ONE ELSE BESIDES HIM. (Mark 12:32)
>
> You believe that God is one. You do well; the demons also believe, and shudder. (James 2:19)

Likewise, we can only observe one light with our unassisted vision. However, close inspection of Polaris reveals God's nature. As Genesis 1:26,27 suggests, God refers to Himself by using plural pronouns in verse 26, saying, "Let Us make man in Our image." But in the very next verse He harmonizes His singular state of existence by saying, "So God created man in His own image," this time using the singular pronoun "His."

Those who concentrate on the New Testament are especially aware of the phenomenon of God's referring to Himself in three different ways. These three stars represent the Father, the Son, and the Holy Spirit. But man is also a composite being. We certainly have a body, but we also have a spirit and a mind/soul. That, however, should come as no surprise, for again, we are made in His image (Genesis 1:27). The triune nature of God is revealed in creation in the Pole star as well as in the construction of man, all of which confirms the biblical text.

Since God is about to return for His bride, she should be readying herself by orienting her life around Him. The movement of the stars and constellations, now around Polaris (God) instead of Draco (the Dragon), is a prophecy forewarning mankind that time is about up. There is a new King in town, and He will call on us to see what we have done with His Son and the book He has given us.

An Ox Is Not a Unicorn!

Unlike modern domestic bulls, the constellation Taurus almost certainly represents a now-extinct relative of domestic cattle, called *rimu* in the Hebrew Scriptures. Rimu is translated as "unicorn" in the Authorized Version and was once thought to be a mythological, one-horned creature. It is now known to be a larger and fiercer type of cattle, which modern translations usually call a "wild ox." Famous for its size and ferocity, it was the prize of great hunters in the records of Egyptian kings such as Tutmose III, and Assyrian kings as well.

Unfortunately, the unicorn mistranslation has been perpetuated in various versions of the Bible. In turn, what can seem like biblical support for the idea that unicorns once existed has been used to supposedly "prove" that the Bible is not accurate. In reality, unicorns are not real animals, extinct or extant, and the Bible does not actually claim anything to the contrary.

3 — Biblical History

Who Were Those Phoenicians?
Some historians have suggested that the Philistines and the inhabitants of Tyre came from the Phoenicians, the Greek name for the seafaring people who colonized the coastlands of the Mediterranean Sea. The Philistines lived in the area now known as Gaza, and they probably do share some bloodlines with the Phoenicians.

The cities of Tyre and Sidon were located in what is known as Lebanon today. However, their inhabitants, and those in the surrounding countryside, were not known as Phoenicians in the Bible. The Israelites recognized them as Canaanites, well known as those who were dwelling in the Promised Land when the Hebrews arrived after escaping from Egypt around 1450 BC. According to Genesis 10, the Canaanites were the descendants of Canaan, the son of Ham. They were the ones whom God cursed when their father, Ham, sinned against his father, Noah.

Romulus and Remus
Some commentators suggest that the tribe of Dan was excluded from the 144,000 in Revelation 7 because their tribe got deeply involved in paganism. In particular, the 17th and 18th chapters of the book of Judges tell the story of the tribe of Dan's involvement with a pagan priest named Micah, whom they installed as their own priest over their own tribe in direct contradiction to all that God had required of them.

It has also been suggested, by ancient historians, that the

origins of Troy and the Trojans find their roots in the tribe of Dan. The original peoples who made up Troy were called "Danaans."

According to ancient legend, Romulus and Remus were twin brothers descended from Troy. One of them founded the city of Rome in 753 BC and named it after himself. Remus, on the other hand, vied with his brother to found a different city on a different hill, but lost the pagan augury (divination) contest by which they decided whose site would be chosen. Remus was not happy with the result; he was killed when he violated the sanctity of his brother's city by leaping over its wall.

About Those Gods and Goddesses

In ancient times, worship often took the form of sacrifices, which included the giving of fruit, animals, money and other valuables, devotion, and often even human children (Leviticus 20:2). Carthaginian parents would honor their gods by ritually sacrificing their young children. Ishtar, the Babylonian earth-goddess, also required child sacrifice to gain her favor. This same goddess is the Ashtoreth, or Astarte, of Scripture.

> The high places which *were* before Jerusalem, which *were* on the right of the mount of destruction which Solomon the king of Israel had built for Ashtoreth the abomination of the Sidonians, and for Chemosh the abomination of Moab, and for Milcom the abomination of the sons of Ammon, the king defiled. (II Kings 23:13)

> Then Samuel spoke to all the house of Israel, saying, "If you return to the LORD with all your heart, remove the foreign gods and the Ashtaroth from among you and direct your hearts to the LORD and serve Him alone; and He will deliver you from the hand of the Philistines." (I Samuel 7:3,4)

36

We derive our modern word "Easter" from Ishtar, one of the biblical variants of the word Ashtoreth. Ashtoreth was the goddess of love and fortune, the Queen of Heaven. She was also the goddess of fertility. Thus we have our "innocent" Easter symbolism involving eggs, and baby chicks, and bunny rabbits.
What's more fertile than a rabbit?

Ishtar, Nun, and other pagan entities were recognized as the gods of *life*, yet required the *destruction* of life to appease them. They also encouraged the use of hallucinogenic drugs to help worshippers enter a more receptive state of consciousness.

Some Things Almost Never End

Recall the relationship between Nimrod, the original king of Babylon, and the original whore of Babylon, Nimrod's mother. She was also his wife. This perverse arrangement was very similar to the relationship we find in Revelation 17, between the whore and the False Messiah. Ishtar (Nimrod's mother), beyond her sexual perversion with her son, had authority over him as well just as the whore has authority over the False Messiah.

Archeologists all over the Mideast have unearthed figurines from ancient times that reveal the same relationship. For example, we find stone bulls, representing Ba'al (who in turn is representing Nimrod), usually with a naked woman sitting on top of the bull, representing Ishtar. We see this exact same relationship in Revelation 17. It depicts a beast again being usurped by a whore, sitting on his back.

But in the end, the beast (or Satan), who has represented

37

himself throughout the ages as Ba'al, ends up destroying the whore. All this gains him the ultimate authority to rule and reign over the entire earth, without her interfering anymore. In the Bible, this whore has represented religious perversion, a substitute and counterfeit for the true religion found in the Bible.

The Babel Babble

Some commentators have confused (1) the babble of Babel with (2) speaking in tongues at Pentecost. But they are not remotely the same thing. In effect, the Babel babble was a curse, inflicted by God because of mankind's rebellion and leading to tremendous confusion among the people who were trying to build a tower that would reach up to heaven so they could challenge God directly. Their God-induced linguistic confusion led to their dispersion all over the world, which was God's way of preventing an even more tragic outcome had they continued their joint construction efforts.

In contrast, those who spoke in tongues on Pentecost were doing God's will by speaking eternal truths in various real-world languages. All of the languages were legitimate even though many of the speakers could not understand what they were saying without the help of translators. Their words absolutely were not "babble" of any kind whatsoever – they were words that God wanted spoken, in the languages God chose to use.

Ironically, these two examples – different as they are – both demonstrate God's infinite ability to use ordinary resources to bring about extraordinary results. No need to smack and smash – in these two cases He simply used our own languages, first to diversify arrogant humans and second to unify willing worshippers.

Amazing.

Naming Rivers and Cities

Because one of the rivers that coursed through the original Garden of Eden was called the Euphrates, some suppose that the Garden of Eden was in the Mesopotamian valley. Today a large river by that name does indeed flow through that valley. But as is common with man, as he migrated all over the earth he also took with him the names of rivers, mountains, and even people that he was familiar with.

This phenomenon can be seen in the naming of cities, states, and even whole regions in America and elsewhere in the world. Common examples would include New York, Moscow (in both Tennessee and Russia), and New England. These names were not given because the folks thought that they were in York, England, or Russia at the time, but because of the fondness they had for the names of things back home.

This same situation may be applicable to the Euphrates. After the flood of Noah's time, people migrated southwest from the Mt. Ararat region and came upon a great river. In memory of their original place of origin they may have named this new river after the one in the Garden. The lost Euphrates — the one that watered the Garden of Eden — flowed eastward from the presence of God. Assuming that God has not changed the location of the place He chooses to dwell in, Jerusalem was, continued to be, and will in the future be the center of

His kingdom. East of Jerusalem, which of course is the Dead Sea's location today, could very well have been the general location of the original Garden of Eden.

And incidentally, it should not be surprising that, because Jerusalem is special in this way, there is such an ongoing fight over this city, with Satan leading the charge.

Common Things Among the Kings

Over the last 6,000 years, seven gentile kingdoms have conquered the land of Israel, along with large portions of the Mideast. In our previous writings we have referred to these kingdoms as the Seven Evil Kingdoms.

Many of the kings who ruled over these evil kingdoms had some things in common. Many thought that they were gods themselves. For example, Alexander the Great thought he was a demigod, born of a woman and a god.

Many of these kings also died in the same way. Some of the details of the deaths of these kings have been lost to history, but several died of syphilis, which we all know is a sexually transmitted disease that results in a very painful and excruciating death. If you've read our *Lost in Translation* series you know that in the seven bowls of judgment that are poured out on the earth, in Revelation 16, each bowl represents one of the symptoms of someone dying from syphilis. So the last kingdom, with its last king, may very well die in the same manner as many of the kings who led these evil empires — syphilis.

The Meaning of Nebuchadnezzar's Name

According to several Bible dictionaries and

commentaries, Nebuchadnezzar "was generally considered the greatest and most powerful of the Babylonian kings." His name literally meant "Prince of the god Nebu," which was the Babylonian name for the false god that the Romans called Mercury and the Greeks called Hermes. The word *chadnez* meant "the god," while *zzar* meant "prince."

According to another authority, *Belteshazzar*, the Babylonian name given to Daniel, possibly meant "Bel is the keeper of secrets." However, another translator suggests that it could have meant "Beltis protects the king," while a third possibility might be "Bel's prince."

Chances are we'll have to ask Daniel himself when we meet him in the hereafter.

4 — Biblical Feasts

Amazing Parallels

In Hebrew culture, the fifty days that elapse between the third and fourth annual feasts, better known as Firstfruits and Shavuot, have long been very special days indeed. In a custom called "Counting the Omer," each individual day is carefully (and often publically) counted, and all religious Jews look forward to the culmination of that count.

Ironically, since most Orthodox Jews do not recognize Yeshua as their promised Messiah, and Christians don't observe the seven feasts of God, neither group recognizes the amazing parallels in Yeshua's life on earth and his impending return. Counting the Omer corresponds to counting up to the day of the coming of the ultimate Groom for His Bride. Indeed, the last trumpet sounds on the 50th day after the resurrection of the two witnesses on Firstfruits.

Christians don't realize that Yeshua was resurrected on Firstfruits, which always occurs on a Sunday per biblical accounting. In so doing He was not moving the Shabbat from Saturday to Sunday, but was recognizing the prophetic fulfillment of the third feast, which is Firstfruits. Then, being ignorant of this fact, many Christians also misunderstand the ancient roots of the next feast. This is called Shavuot in the Bible, but is also known in the Christian world as Pentecost.

Pentecost occurs 50 days after Shavuot. It is the Christian Church today that honors this day as the coming of the spirit of God to dwell in man. However, its ancient biblical moorings inform us that this was the day that God gave the Law to His people. 1 Corinthians 2 explains that the purpose of the Spirit of God was to lead us into all truth. Truth in the Bible is always referred back to God's principles for holy living. These principles are outlined in the Torah and are called God's Law. This is delineated throughout the Bible, including the New Testament.

On Firstfruits the Israelites passed safely through the Red Sea and were saved from the Egyptians. Fifty days later, on Shavuot, they received the Torah, God's marriage contract with us, amid the loud sound of the shofar and God's thundering voice.

Yeshua was resurrected on the feast of Firstfruits. Fifty days later the Holy Spirit came on Shavuot. The two witnesses of Revelation 11 may very well be resurrected on Firstfruits. Fifty days later the last trumpet will sound on Shavuot, and Yeshua will return in the clouds for His Bride.

Also, on ancient Shavuot celebrations the primary focal point of this feast was the celebration at the temple and the offering of two loaves of leavened bread. Here, the bread represented life and the leavening in the bread represented an increase in holiness rather than representing an increase of sin as it does in the feast of Unleavened Bread. And as Paul explained, that holiness is procured by running the race to win the crown. A believer's responsibility is to become holy by integrating God's principles for holy living into their lives, thereby causing their life to increase, or leaven.

Why Some Do Not Tithe

Some people offer the excuse that they do not tithe because, by the end of the month, just before the next payday, they don't have enough money left to give Him His portion. There is just not enough available after paying all the bills and other important expenses.

The principles of the feast of Firstfruits models how we should give to God. We offer Him the first of our income, not the last. In other words, we make sure that our account with heaven is paid first. This obligation is the most important expense that we have. Then we pay our other obligations, trusting in Him to provide enough to get us to our next harvest, or paycheck.

As Malachi assures us, obedience to God guarantees His blessing and protection:

> "Bring the whole tithe into the storehouse, so that there may be food in My house, and test Me now in this," says the LORD of hosts, "if I will not open for you the windows of heaven and pour out for you a blessing until it overflows." (Malachi 3:10)

God's Infinite Patience

The thousand-year reign offers us one more beautiful picture showing how God gives people every possible opportunity to choose to serve Him, as exemplified by Rosh Hashanah (Feast of Trumpets) and Yom Kippur (Day of Atonement).

Rosh Hashanah was recognized as a celebration for those who had their names written in the Book of Life. Yom Kippur, which occurs ten days later, figuratively represents the thousand-year reign and enables God to extend to mankind another period of time during which they can get it right and correct their lives. However, the end of this final ten-day period absolutely terminates their final chance to get their names rewritten in the Book of Life. The thousand-year reign is terminated by the great White Throne Judgment, when the Book of Life is opened and mankind is judged one last time.

The Four Seasons

Passover will always fall in the spring. So, that means that it will always fall on or after March 21st in the northern hemisphere. This date on the Gregorian calendar is the spring equinox, the first day of spring and the halfway point in our sky that the sun appears to reach.

Each year on December 21 the sun transverses the lowest course in the southern sky. On June 21 it reaches the highest course overhead. These dates are referred to as the winter solstice and the summer solstice respectively. They also denote the beginning of each of these seasons as well. Of course, the fall equinox then falls on September 21, which marks the first day of fall.

Because the Hebrew calendar is lunar, the first of the month always starts on the sighting of the first sliver of the new moon per God's instructions. Sometimes there is a need for a leap year. In the case of our current calendar, we use a leap day about every four years to keep our calendar in sync with the seasons.

The ancient Hebrews used a leap month. They would add a whole month just before the start of Nisan 1, which was the beginning of their new year. This additional month would be added when they determined that on Nisan 1 they were still more than 14 days from the spring equinox. They were aware that God had instructed them that Passover, which occurred on Nisan 14, had to fall in the spring.

The ancients were always aware of how many days were left in any of the four seasons and were able to predict the beginning of the next. Seven leap months occur in about every 19 years.

Did Yeshua Honor the Feasts?

The Bible makes it clear that Yeshua Himself honored the seven feasts ordained by God the Father. He even went to the temple on Hanukkah, a manmade feast still celebrated by the Jews today which Yeshua also considered worthy of remembrance. But the story does not end there.

Four significant events in the earthly life of Yeshua occurred on four of the seven biblical feast days — His death on *Passover*, His time in the tomb on *Unleavened Bread*, His resurrection on *Firstfruits*, and His sending of the Holy Spirit on *Shavuot* (known to modern believers as *Pentecost*).

Every bit of evidence that we have also suggests that He was born in the fall on *Succoth*, which would raise the above four to five. Clearly those well-known shepherds would not have been "abiding in the fields" in the middle of the winter, on the 25th of the modern month of December. Those same flocks were always brought down to lower elevations. There they would feed off the land without having to endure the winter temperatures and snow storms of the higher elevations.

The biblical text also strongly hints that Succoth will end the thousand-year reign, ushering in the great white throne judgment. In memory of the concept of the feast of Succoth, God will then begin his dwelling with man on earth once again.

Two more of the seven feasts, yet to be associated with Yeshua, would be *Rosh Hashanah* and *Yom Kippur*. Speculation about the Feast of Trumpets is especially interesting, because that feast day was known idiomatically, in ancient Hebrew, as "the day and the hour of which no man knows." This designation came about because the ancients did not have the advantage of modern astronomical technology. Thus the Feast of Trumpets officially began on the first day of the month of *Tishri*, when two or more witnesses were able to confirm before the Sanhedrin in Jerusalem that they had personally observed the new moon in the evening sky.

Once the beginning of the feast day was officially established, the news was communicated by a series of signal fires. The first one was built on the western wall of Jerusalem and then duplicated on the tops of hills in a series of bonfires that moved from the east to the west, alerting the whole nation of Israel. This was accompanied by trumpet blasts, also called *thunders*, on the ancient ram's horn trumpets known as shofars. The shofar blasts officially summoned the head of each family to come immediately to the temple.

In the 24th chapter of Matthew, when Yeshua's disciples

asked when He would be coming back, among other things He said the following: "For as lightning that comes from the east is visible even in the west, so will be the coming of the Son of Man" (Matthew 24:27). This verse is a direct reference to the signal fires mentioned above, as they moved from one hill to the next to alert the people. Because Jerusalem was in the eastern portion of Israel, the fires would travel down toward the Mediterranean sea coast to the west.

That would bring the total to six out of seven, with only Yom Kippur to go. And that, of course, would be the Day of Judgment as well as the day of Yeshua's wedding.

Two More Holidays
In addition to the basic feasts as mentioned previously, most observant Jews celebrate at least two additional annual holidays. However, both of these might be called "manmade" as opposed to "ordained by God."

The oldest of the two, *Purim*, was established to celebrate the victory of Queen Esther and her uncle Mordecai over their tormentor, Haman, who plotted to kill all the Jews in the Persian kingdom. This is a lesson in how our disobedience can affect us in the long term.

Haman was a descendent of the Amalekites. The Amalekites were brought under judgment by God but were not dealt with as God directed Saul, the King of Israel, to do more than 500 years earlier. Because of Saul's disobedience Haman's ancestors were allowed to live, thus eventually bringing Haman into the picture. However, God used this entire story to emphasize that even when we sin He can still save us from its

49

consequences. In the nick of time God provided a way out from Haman's evil schemes and saved His people.

The second of these manmade feasts, *Hanukkah* is an eight-day Jewish festival established to celebrate the rededication of the Temple in Jerusalem at the successful end of the Maccabean revolt against the Jews' Syrian/Seleucid oppressors, circa 165 BC. This holiday was established after Antiochus Epiphanies, the Seleucid king, was defeated by the ragtag armies of the Jews.

As soon as they retook their Temple in Jerusalem the Jews of that era began to repair and cleanse the house of God. They then discovered that they had only enough oil to light the menorah, their seven-light lamp stand, for one day. The miracle occurred when this bit of oil lasted for eight full days. This allowed the Hebrews enough time to make a new batch of oil.

This feast is celebrated as a remembrance of our thankfulness for God's blessing and His deliverance of our ancestors during their time of trouble. Antiochus was completely defeated and died unexpectedly a few years later.

Hanukkah is sometimes called the "Jewish Christmas" because it usually occurs during the Christmas season. It also involves giving gifts to your loved ones on each of the eight days.

5 — From a Hebraic Perspective

Who Sinned: Adam or Eve?

Some propose that Eve was the first sinner, the one who fell from God's grace first and was then joined later on by Adam, after she convinced him to eat of the forbidden fruit as well. In actuality, Eve didn't really "sin" at all as it's defined in the Bible. Adam did! The primary meaning for the Hebrew word for "sin" means "to rebel" while knowing God's truth but deciding not to honor it anyway. Eve's error was that she was deceived and believed the lie that Satan told her. There was no rebellion in Eve's heart; she fell because she bought into the lie.

On the other hand, Adam truly sinned. In Hebrew the word for "sin" means to rebel. Once Eve had been deceived into believing the lie, Adam with full knowledge discovered what had happened, rebelled against God, and joined in with his wife. Therefore, he turned his face away from God, towards rebellion, on purpose. He clearly knew that God had instructed him not to eat from the tree of the knowledge of Good and Evil, but he chose to love his wife more than he loved God.

That tendency and condition continues even today. Sometimes with very good intentions we find ourselves rebelling against God. Others, with good intentions as well, can be fooled by circumstances into disobeying God with no intention in their heart to actually rebel.

This is why the biblical text, in many places, instructs us to know God's word. God's word is our compass and our rudder, not our feelings or the circumstances we find

51

ourselves in.

The foundation of the Bible is Torah, the first five books which contain God's principles for holy living. One of the meanings of Torah is "to hit the mark." Every day, if we know what Torah says we should be attempting to line up our lives in conformity with God's principles for holy living, so we literally "live out" the word of God.

A Little Word with a Big Story

The rabbis believe that God used Hebrew to speak the universe into existence, and the very first sentence of the Bible provides quite a bit of evidence. Genesis 1:1 consists of seven Hebrew words, the fourth of which is the Hebrew word *et*, formed by the first and last letters of the Hebrew alephbet, *aleph* and *tav*. This little word strongly suggests that God is identifying Himself in the very first sentence of His Word as the *controller of the beginning and the end and everything in between.* Just as many linguists now believe that Hebrew is the true forerunner of all other languages, Hebrew also appears to be God's native language as well – His Mother-Father tongue.

If you look at any Hebrew Interlinear Bible you will see that *et* never gets translated. Why does this word have no English equivalent? Because *et* is a grammatical marker which functions like a road sign to tell the reader that a *definite direct object lies just ahead.* For example, "I ate the apple" in Hebrew would be "I ate *et* the apple." "I hit the ball" would be "I hit *et* the ball."

How interesting that the author of the Hebrew language would place within the grammar of the language itself an indispensable word like *et,* whose very presence continually reminds us that He should be the ultimate *definite direct object* of all our words and all our actions.

Whatever we do, in word or deed, should be done unto Him.

Ten Righteous People

When Abraham bartered with God in Genesis 18, to spare Sodom and Gomorrah if enough righteous people could be found there, he started at fifty and worked his way down to ten. Some people wonder why Abraham stopped at ten and have even accused him of not being persistent enough, suggesting that God might have been willing to go down to five, or three, or even two.

In our society we embrace the concept of a quorum of ten, which reflects the Hebrew concept of what the number ten means. Ten, in Hebrew, is the symbol for righteous government. Abraham knew that ten righteous people could provide a righteous covering/government over a city or a nation. Conversely, he would have known equally well that if he didn't have ten righteous people (i.e., a righteous government) there simply would not be any hope for that city.

About Those Judgments

Many suggest that the Bible doesn't present itself in a coherent, logical progression of thought. Rather they propose that it's a jumbled collection of books that have been collected over time, with no particular order or structure. However, what we find via a closer look is the exact opposite.

One example would be that at the beginning of the Bible,

in the first five books, God clearly promises to His people that, if they do well and listen to his instructions, they will be blessed. However, if they ignore His instructions they will be cursed, and the curses we find at the very beginning of the Bible are very specifically delineated as are the blessings.

What do you suppose we find at the end of the Bible? These very same blessings and curses are being poured out on those people who deserve them. So, if you've done poorly you've earned curses, and the book of Revelation talks about the End Time, and the coming apocalyptic events that will befall mankind. If you compare those curses in the book of Revelation with the promised curses for disobeying God way back at the beginning of the book, they are the same.

And the same is true of the blessings.

To Cover or Uncover the Head

For hundreds of years Christianity has done precisely the opposite of what the Jews do and has insisted that men remove all head coverings when they came into a church. Supposedly they do so out of respect for God, although nothing in the Bible suggests such a thing, including the 11th chapter of 1 Corinthians. This particular passage refers to the veils that prostitutes wore in Paul's day to show their availability. Prostitutes in Greek society were soliciting relationships with their own gods and were actually coming into synagogue services trying to win converts.

Nowadays, of course, the Christian custom of uncovering the head has largely disappeared. In many modern churches you can find young men wearing baseball caps, skull-tight scarves, and even fedoras.

Nonetheless, the origin of the custom of uncovering the head, in the Christian church, came about because of Roman persecution of the Gentilic portion of the Sect of the Nazarenes. The early congregations were composed of both Jews and Gentiles. When the Romans outlawed Judaism, which then included Gentile believers, the Gentiles chose to do everything they could to stop looking like Jews. Thus they switched their wedding rings from the right to the left hand (even though the right hand has always been the honored hand), stopped celebrating the Old Testament feasts, switched the Sabbath from Saturday to Sunday, and took their kippahs off. Eventually, all these newer things (and others as well) became "honored customs" even as they replaced the original practices of which they were now complete opposites.

In contrast, the opposite Jewish custom of always covering the head, based on the Bible, the Talmud, and archeological evidence, still prevails within both traditional and Messianic Judaism.

The Book of Life
From the foundations of the earth, God wrote our names in His Book of Life. In Hebrew thought – and also, incidentally, in American Indian (i.e., Native American) thought as well – our names alone represent something important about us.

This is true because our names were given to us and written down by God even as He conceived His individual plan for each of our lives — encompassing what we should do, what we should learn, how (and perhaps whom) we should love, what impact we should have on others during our lifetimes, and what lasting effect we should leave behind.

Having thus identified us He will then look to these descriptions to see if there is anyone's life within His Book with which our set of accomplishments can be identified. Sometimes the only part of our life that is in the book is the record of our salvation. That's a major positive but that is not, however, God's entire end game plan for us.

The point is, there is more to being a child of the kingdom of God than just salvation. God has recorded a description of each one of us that includes all of our responsibilities in life. They are described in the biblical text with the word "holiness," and holiness is defined in the Bible as following God's principles.

Baptism and Communion
The modern Christian understanding of baptism and communion have both been corrupted when compared to their ancient biblical roots. The original *mikveh* (the forerunner of modern baptism) involved standing in a river, facing the current, and bowing forward, both literally and symbolically, toward the water's source. That source was recognized as God Himself, because He is the source of all life. One of the metaphorical understandings of water, in the Bible, is "life." In so bowing down in the water, one is prostrating himself as a symbol of the humility and submission in the heart that one is offering, literally, to God.

In contrast, modern full-body baptism typically involves being "saved from drowning in sin" by falling backwards into the literal "arms of the church" as wielded by a priest or a pastor. Some churches also teach that being baptized more than once is inappropriate – or downright wrong.

In contrast, the ancient Jews would mikveh frequently as instructed by the word of God. The priests did so before they went into the inner court. Jewish women did so at the end of every menstrual period, as a way of ritually purifying themselves. Like any other legitimate rabbi, Yeshua Himself also did so just prior to beginning his active ministry.

What the modern church now calls "communion" is based on the original Passover/Last Supper meal at which Yeshua washed His disciples feet then shared bread and wine with them. All three of these were based on the three covenants leading up to betrothal. Washing His disciples feet mirrored the sandal (inheritance) covenant. Eating the bread together mirrored the salt (friendship) covenant. Drinking the wine mirrored blood (servant) covenant, which Yeshua reinforced by noting that this was the last cup of wine He would share with His people before coming back for His Bride.

So, when we take communion today what we should be doing, along with recognizing the price that was paid for our sins on the Cross, by our Saviour, is to recall and recommit ourselves to these three covenants. When we take the wine (the blood) we are recommitting ourselves to be obedient to God's laws. When we eat the bread we are recommitting ourselves to develop further our relationship with God, as we would with anyone else that we knew as more than just an acquaintance.

In addition, since communion is really an echo of Passover, we should recall that we are also recommitting ourselves to the inheritance covenant. This would require that we manage our lives and the responsibilities that God has given us in such a way that we are mindful, at all times, of the desires that God wants to accomplish in His kingdom. In fact, we should be acting like ambassadors for His kingdom. Communion takes on a much more intimate and covenantal idea when understood from the original source, the Bible, rather than what it has become when those ancient ideals are stripped away.

Why Didn't Adam and Eve Die?

Lots of people claim that the Genesis text is wrong, because obviously Adam and Eve did not die when they ate the forbidden fruit. But being separated from God encompassed the concept of death from an Hebraic perspective, not what physical death involved from a western perspective. Here, once sin entered the world it separated man from God, and therefore they literally "died" on the day they sinned because they were separated from Him.

Is the "Good News" Really New?

Many people believe that the concept of "good news" is a new concept presented for the first time within the New Testament (i.e., the *B'rit Hadashah*). On the contrary, it's an ancient concept presented by God in the Old Testament, hundreds of years prior to the first century AD.

As within all the prophetic writings, the pattern here is

the same. God is angry with His people for the evil they're embracing and the sins they're committing. He brings judgment, punishment, and hardship. Then He relents, has mercy, and says that He is going to return to His people and restore them. This is the good news!

And yes, mankind has a part to play in the restoration as well. God is coming for those who, in spite of their sin, have been attentive to His call.

> Get yourself up on a high mountain,
> O Zion, bearer of good news,
> Lift up your voice mightily,
> O Jerusalem, bearer of good news;
> Lift *it* up, do not fear.
> Say to the cities of Judah,
> "Here is your God!" (Isaiah 40:9)

> Formerly *I said* to Zion, 'Behold, here they are.'
> And to Jerusalem, 'I will give a messenger of good news.'
> (Isaiah 41:27)

> How lovely on the mountains
> Are the feet of him who brings good news,
> Who announces]peace
> And brings good news of happiness,
> Who announces salvation,
> *And* says to Zion, "Your God reigns! (Isaiah 52:7)

> The Spirit of the Lord GOD is upon me,
> Because the LORD has anointed me
> To bring good news to the afflicted;
> He has sent me to bind up the brokenhearted,
> To proclaim liberty to captives
> And freedom to prisoners. (Isaiah 61:1)

> "A multitude of camels will cover you,
> The young camels of Midian and Ephah;

All those from Sheba will come;
They will bring gold and frankincense,
And will bear good news of the praises of the LORD. (Isaiah 60:6)

Behold, on the mountains the feet of him who brings good news,
Who announces peace!
Celebrate your feasts, O Judah;
Pay your vows.
For never again will the wicked one pass through you;
He is cut off completely. (Nahum 1:15)

The Three Levels of Hell

Scripture contains three words that describe the three levels of the underworld, or the "afterlife" for the wicked. The first is *Sheol* (the grave); the second is *Gehenna* (a place of fiery torment, the lake of fire, i.e., hell), and the third is *Abaddon* (the abyss).

Are there levels in heaven as well, that are reflected by the different kinds of covenant? We believe that God will reward those who have done well with the most valuable thing that God can give: relationship, proximity, and resulting authority over His creation.

What Does the Word "Israel" Mean?

The ancients, especially the eastern nations (including the Hebrews), used names to describe some interesting event or attribute connected to the person in question. God used this same idea when he named the Hebrews *Israel*. In Hebrew, *Israel* means *the prince or warrior of God*. Therefore, those who are His should act their part, representing the King and realizing they have responsibilities and work to do for Him. In the end, God is going to give everybody a new name! And this name will reflect the work and accomplishments that we have made during our lives on Earth. Thus the efforts that we make now, in the kingdom of God, will reflect on our heavenly identity.

What's in a Name?

The world knows Him as "Jesus Christ." But while He lived here on earth He was known by the Hebrew name his mother gave Him at His birth. As we explained in Volume 1 of the *Lost in Translation* series, in Matthew 1:21 an angel of the Lord told the virgin Mary (actually, in both Hebrew and English her name would be *Miriam*, or *Miryam* as it's sometimes transliterated) to name her unborn child *Yeshua*, which means "I am Salvation." Mary/Miriam then used that name whenever she called her son in for lunch.

In the 2,000 years since Yeshua's birth, any number of complicated explanations have come along to explain how "Yeshua" became "Jesus Christ." Here's what we consider the most likely sequence:

Hebrew		Greek		Latin		English
Yeshua	=	**Iesous**	=	**Jesu**	=	**Jesus**

To the above we would add only one additional point. The "Christ" portion comes from the Greek word "Christos," a title that was often applied to Olympic athletes, meaning "godlike." "Jesus Christ" thus becomes a combination of two separate Latin and Greek words, neither of which Yeshua was ever known by in His life on earth.

61

To Abolish or Fulfill?

Most people seem to agree that the passage below, in Matthew, is actually saying that God didn't come to abolish the law, but to fulfill it:

> "Do not think that I came to abolish the Law or the Prophets; I did not come to abolish but to fulfill. For truly I say to you, until heaven and earth pass away, not the smallest letter or stroke shall pass from the Law until all is accomplished. Whoever then annuls one of the least of these commandments, and teaches others to do the same, shall be called least in the kingdom of heaven; but whoever keeps and teaches them, he shall be called great in the kingdom of heaven." (Matthew 5:17-19)

However, many other people also claim that in the "fulfilling" of the law He "completed" it, thereby making it null and void. This idea proposes that what Yeshua is really saying is, "I didn't come to abolish the law, but to abolish the law!" Which, of course, makes no sense at all.

The Greek word for fulfill is *plaroo*. This word means to "make full, to fill up." It is used in the Septuagint for the Hebrew word *mala*. This word complements its Greek counterpart because it also means "to fill, to make full." But it does not mean "to terminate."

Therefore, Yeshua is saying here that the goal of His life on earth was (and still is) to bring a full and complete understanding of His Word to all of mankind, and to fulfill the prophecies foretelling His first coming.

All of this information was given by God in the Old Testament prior to Yeshua's birth in Bethlehem. Nothing in His words here in Matthew is meant to convey the idea that His life and death on earth, some 2,000 years ago, was meant to "terminate" anything, except Satan's authority over us due to our sin.

God never meant to give mankind two separate plans yielding two separate paths into His eternal presence. As Hebrews 13:8 tells us, "Jesus Christ is the same yesterday and today and forever." Couldn't be any plainer.

However, some people propose that there were in fact two plans, with the Old Testament presenting "Plan 1," which was to procure salvation by following Torah. They then propose that the New Testament provided "Plan 2," another way to salvation via Yeshua's death on the cross.

This is not at all correct. There has always been one and only one plan. Abraham, as well as all people who lived after the death and resurrection of Yeshua, have always been invited into the kingdom of God via their faith. The law, or "Torah," was always presented as a means for establishing a proper relationship with both God and mankind, not for salvation itself. That came only through faith.

What Is it About Blood?

We often think that the shed blood saves us from our sins. However, it is not actually the blood itself that makes the difference — it's the life or soul *within* the blood. Leviticus 17:11 states.

> For the life of the flesh is in the blood, and I have given it to you on the altar to make atonement for your souls; for it is the blood by reason of the life that makes atonement.

Thus Yeshua gave up His life's blood on the Cross on our behalf. The Hebrew word in the above verse for *life* and for *soul* is the same. It is the word *nephesh*. So, as the verse says, it was not the *blood* that made the atonement for your soul, it was the soul (or *nephesh*) that was *in* the blood that made the atonement.

This word nephesh can be translated as "life," "creature," and sometimes as "soul." Its first occurrence comes in

Genesis 1:21:

> God created the great sea monsters and every living *creature* that moves, with which the waters swarmed after their kind, and every winged bird after its kind; and God saw that it was good.

Nephesh is the underlying Hebrew word translated above as "creature." That is certainly a correct choice to describe various living animals. However, let's take a look at another verse in Genesis 2:7:

> Then the LORD God formed man of dust from the ground, and breathed into his nostrils the breath of life; and man became a living being.

This verse describes the creation of man rather than animals. The underlying Hebrew word for "being" is the same word, *nephesh*, used back in Genesis 1:21 where it was translated as "creature."

Unfortunately, readers do not get a clear understanding of what God is trying to tell us because the translators are being inconsistent. What God is conveying in both of these verses is that He put a soul in all living creatures, including mankind. It is this very soul that must be given up as payment for sin.

The difference between man and the animals does not

reside in the type of souls but in how God created them. Animal souls were created by the spoken word of God. They became living by the very words that came out of His mouth. On the other hand, man became a living soul through the breath of life that came from the mouth of God.

The Hebrew words for "breath of life" are *chi neshmah.* *Neshmah* is a word commonly used to mean "Spirit of God" in Hebrew. So, this verse supports the rabbinical idea that a bit of God Himself dwells within each person.

Thus the difference is relatively simple. God created the animal souls by His spoken word, but He created mankind's souls by placing a bit of Himself in each person. God was making a very big point here, which is commonly missed. Man is very special to God. Yes, he is much more important than the animals, although God loves and cares for them as well. That's why it is our job to manage and protect them.

Baptism vs. Mikveh

In conjunction with the shopworn old premise that the New Testament presents new concepts and themes, and support for a new religion, baptism is thought of by many as a "Christian" concept unrelated to anything in the Old Testament. However, as we are finding, the Bible is actually one continuous presentation of a godly lifestyle, leading to holiness.

Because, as the Bible reveals, God's overall plan for us spans the entire life cycle of mankind on earth, giving us a panoramic view of time and history. This history includes the part yet in our future, giving us hope that our destinies do not just include death but also include life after death and the coming of our Creator.

Contrary to what many Christians have been taught — and in total synch with the summary above — baptism is a very old idea with deep roots in the Old Testament. One of the instructions given to Moses when he was setting up the Tabernacle included what many might call a "wash basin." This bronze laver was set between the bronze altar and the Tent of Meeting. Before anyone could enter the Inner court of the Tent of Meeting they had to wash themselves. This duty was required upon pain of death.

Thus, before a priest could approach the presence of God he needed to analyze himself, inwardly and outwardly, then purify himself via the cleansing qualities of water. God presents the idea that we are all priests, serving Him in our daily lives. The parallel is stark. As we approach God we also should present ourselves to Him as holy, humble, and repentant.

Ritual purity is described as full immersion in water. The word *mikveh*, in Hebrew, is used to describe a place where water flows together. The Hebrew baptism/mikveh was done in fresh, flowing water with the person facing the source of the flow. He would then bow forward, completely immersing himself in the moving water. The idea here is that God is the source of our life, which the flowing water represents. As we humble ourselves in front of Him, the life-giving purity washes away the impurities present in our lives due to our poor choices.

Of course, all of these rituals should only be a

representation of what is going on inside our minds and hearts. Without our heartfelt commitments and decisions to act properly, all rote rituals are just water over the dam.

The Shepherd Who Breaks Down the Walls

In the King James translation of Matthew 11:11–12 we find the following.

> Verily I say unto you, Among them that are born of women there hath not risen a greater than John the Baptist: notwithstanding he that is least in the kingdom of heaven is greater than he. And from the days of John the Baptist until now the kingdom of heaven suffereth violence, and the violent take it by force.

Various commentators have misinterpreted the last sentence, above, for hundreds of years. The Amplified Bible even adds the words "as a precious prize – a share in the heavenly kingdom is sought with most ardent zeal and intense exertion" to the end of it. But in reality, these verses refer directly to a passage found in Micah 2:12–13:

> I will surely assemble, O Jacob, all of thee; I will surely gather the remnant of Israel; I will put them together as the sheep of Bozrah, as the flock in the midst of their fold: they shall make great noise by reason of the multitude of men. The breaker is come up before them: they have broken up, and have passed through the gate, and are gone out by it: and their king shall pass before them, and the LORD on the head of them. (KJV)

In the original Hebrew, the word translated as "breaker" is *peretz*, meaning either a shepherd who breaks boundaries to release his sheep ("breaching forth") or a woman going into labor (a birthing term).

Typically, an ancient Hebrew shepherd penned his sheep up each night, within an enclosure made of rocks. When it came time to let them loose in the morning, the shepherd (i.e., the "breaker") would knock out some of the stones in the wall with his staff. The sheep themselves would then expand the breach in the process of escaping, as they were set free or "birthed."

In a similar way, this passage explains that, in response to Yeshua, the Kingdom of Heaven is "bursting forth." It is clearly a Messianic reference; Yeshua is saying, "I smashed the rock out and birthed you forth; I am the shepherd who breaks down the walls and sets you free."

When the Greek words that are commonly translated as "the kingdom of heaven suffereth violence, and the violent take it by force" are translated back into what was undoubtedly the original Hebrew, they become an idiomatic expression (as described above) that lines up perfectly with what Micah was saying.

In other words, the whole thing makes no sense at all in the standard Hebrew-to-Greek-to-English sequence. Only when the Greek is translated directly back into Hebrew, and then directly into English, does it ring true.

How to Determine Whether a Dream, a Vision, a Feeling, or an Impression Has Merit

1) Does it line up with God's Word? (Deuteronomy 13:1–4)
2) Does the messenger have a history of having his

messages come true? (Deuteronomy 18:22)

3) Does the messenger speak in the name of other gods? (Deuteronomy 18:20)

4) Is the messenger himself living an exemplary life? Is he attempting to follow the ways of God? (Jeremiah 23:10,14)

5) Is the messenger countering the Word of God? For example, is he speaking blessings when no blessing has been earned, when in fact the Bible promised a curse for doing such things or behaving in such a manner? (Jeremiah 23:17)

6) Does the word come in an orderly manner or environment? (1 Corinthians 14:37-40)

Good News for All!

We are often struck with the topic in the New Testament concerning "Good News." In our churches today this good news is sometimes presented in a way that implies that it is something new; maybe even something that was not expected. What is this good news? And is it something never spoken about before?

First of all, this good news is all about the coming of the Messiah, Yeshua. But more important, it tells us that His accomplishments during His life here on earth have brought us salvation through faith. As Paul explained:

> . . . if you confess with your mouth Jesus *as* Lord, and believe in your heart that God raised Him from the dead, you will be saved; 10 for with the heart a person believes, resulting in righteousness, and with the mouth he confesses, resulting in salvation. (Romans 10:9–10)

What is missing from many pastoral sermons, however,

is that the good news spoken about in Romans and many other places in the New Testament is actually a continuation of a similar theme in the Old Testament. In fact, the Romans 10 passage that refers to this good news, in verse 15, is quoting Isaiah 52:7 as revealed below:

> How will they preach unless they are sent? Just as it is written, "HOW BEAUTIFUL ARE THE FEET OF THOSE WHO BRING GOOD NEWS OF GOOD THINGS!" (Romans 10:15)
> How lovely on the mountains Are the feet of him who brings good news,
> Who announces peace And brings good news of happiness,
> Who announces salvation, *And* says to Zion, "Your God reigns!" (Isaiah 52:7)

Here in Isaiah the original Hebrew word for good news is *basar* and usually gets translated as "glad tidings." This is the Hebrew source word for the Greek word we find in the Septuagint and the New Testament, for good news.

Unfortunately, the translators are not consistent with their English word choices and blur this continuity. God, from ancient times, has given mankind hope: That He would come someday and take away the sins of the world. This has been the good news for all mankind, from Genesis to the book of Revelation.

6 — Hebrew Language and Pictographs

What's the Deal With "Grace"?

Revelation 4:8 pronounces that the Lord God Almighty is holy when it proclaims:

> Each of the four living creatures had six wings and was covered with eyes all around, even under his wings. Day and night they never stop saying: "Holy, holy, holy is the Lord God Almighty, who was, and is, and is to come." (NIV:

In other words, God thinks holy thoughts, He does holy deeds, and He has holy motives. In Hebrew, the word for holy is *kadosh* and is spelled *koof/vav/dalet/shin.* The underlying pictography says to "put in the past the covenant pathway that consumes you." Thus, when we disobey God and reject His holiness we actually enter into a destructive counter-covenant with the Adversary. This counter-covenant is negated and replaced with a better covenant, with God, when we repent, conforming our ways to His will. I Peter 1:13–15 says:

> [13]Therefore, prepare your minds for action; be self-controlled; set your hope fully   on the grace to be given you when Jesus Christ is revealed. [14]As obedient children, do not conform to the evil desires you had when you lived in ignorance. [15]But just as he who called you is holy, so be holy in all you do; [16]for it is written: "Be holy, because I am holy." (NIV)

So what, then, is God's standard for holiness? We are admonished also to be holy in several passages in Torah, including the following:

> "For I am the LORD your God. Consecrate yourselves therefore, and be holy, for I am holy. And you shall not make yourselves unclean with any of the swarming things that swarm on the earth." (Leviticus 11:44)

> "Speak to all the congregation of the sons of Israel and say to them, 'You shall be holy, for I the LORD your God am holy.'" (Leviticus 19:2)

> 'Thus you are to be holy to Me, for I the LORD am holy; and I have set you apart from the peoples to be Mine." (Leviticus 20:26)

So what, then, is God's standard for holiness?

These texts were among the original instructions about being holy and tell us what holiness is all about. Nonetheless, some commentators suggest that the Old Testament principles have been abolished because we now live under grace.

Actually, we do live under grace. But in truth, God's people have *always* lived under grace, because the sacrificial system was nothing more nor less than a forward-looking memorial to the time when Yeshua Himself would literally become the sacrificial Lamb for all of mankind. He didn't save just those who arrived on earth after His death – He saved ALL believers, since the beginning of time, who put their faith in God and lived their lives accordingly.

The Gog Pictograph

In Ezekiel, chapter 38, we find a reference to Gog and Magog that many believe is a reference to the land of Russia and its rulers. The Hebrew letters that spell the word *Gog* are *gimel/vav/gimel*. The pictographic understanding of these letters is to "lift up the covenant of pride."

This is an extremely fitting description of Russia and its leaders. As dogmatic atheists, the Russian leaders have been opposed to religion of any sort, but especially to Christianity and Judaism. They have opposed any representation of God, the church, or any other organizations that would spread any ideas about the Christian and/or Jewish Bible in the nations they have ruled over. They have killed and persecuted millions of people during the last 100 years, destroying their places of worship by turning them into museums or using them in any way other than the original purposes intended by their builders.

The Hebrew letters that spell the word *Magog* are *mem/gimel/vav/gimel*. The pictographic meaning here is to "lift up the covenant of pride *and chaos*." The word Magog can also refer to the location where the people of Gog live, which is "the land of Gog."

Certainly the history of Russia illustrates what happens when you manage your life and country without including God and His core values. Abuse, death camps, utter disregard for human life and freedom, and management by fear are all the results of a prideful, chaotic, godless society.

Is it a Decan or a Deacon?
Many modern scholars are coming to the conclusion that Hebrew was the original language from which all other languages evolved. This, of course, is no surprise to Jewish scribes who were students of the Tanach. From

ancient times they proposed that the language with which God spoke the universe into existence was Hebrew.

However, at the Tower of Babel God intentionally created all the other languages from which every language spoken today has evolved. When modern scholars track our current languages back in time, in geographical terms they end up in Iraq, the exact location of the Tower of Babel. Most Hebrew scholars also propose that God will restore the knowledge of this original language when He comes back. God refers to this language as "pure" in Zephaniah 3:9.

Supporting the idea that Hebrew was the original language, the names of many of the animals only mean something in Hebrew. For example, the word for elephant, in Hebrew, is spelled *pel/yod/lamed.* The Hebrew pictographic meaning of these Hebrew letters describes an animal that has a long rod that speaks and does work. Recall that Adam was the one who, at the direction of God, gave names to all the different animals. So, when he observed the elephant he described its unique trunk.

The migrations of people groups all over the globe all began in the Middle East. Even the origins of domesticated grapevines all lead us back to Turkey. Remember, Noah planted the first grape vineyards after the flood near mountains of Ararat, which is in (or near) Turkey.

Shem or Melchizedek

Among Hebrew scholars, Shem (son of Noah) is

known later in the biblical text as Melchizedek, the king of Salem.

> And Melchizedek king of Salem brought out bread and wine; now he was a priest of God Most High. (Genesis 14:18)

Jerusalem and Salem are the same city. The word *Jerusalem* is made up of two Hebrew words. *Salem* is better known in its other pronunciation, "shalom," which means "peace." It is commonly used by Jews today to greet someone. It means "hello," or "peace be to you."

Jeru, the first part of Jerusalem, is thought to mean "men" or "people," or perhaps "foundation" or "habitation." It is appropriate, then, that Jerusalem will be the dwelling place of the coming King, who will truly be the foundation for peace on earth for all mankind.

There are amplifications with respect to the meaning of Jerusalem. Dr. Danny Ben-Gigi proposes the following:

> *Yir-oo-shalem* is made of two words: *yir-oo* and *shalem*. The root of the word *yir-oo* means: "They will see" or "They will feel awe." "Shalem" means "complete, whole." "They will see completeness," or "feel the awe of wholeness" is the meaning of the name Jerusalem.

Maybe this is why everyone is fighting over this city. Doesn't everyone want to be restored back to wholeness, to recover from the consequences of sin and to have peace in their lives?

The First, the Strong, and the Mighty
The first letter of the Hebrew alephbet is *aleph*. In ancient times, when the Torah was written, this letter

took the form of the head of a bull. It is not accidental that its pictographic meaning is "first, strong, and mighty."

The last of the Hebrew letters is *tav*. This letter was drawn in the form of a cross. Pictographically it meant "the sign of the covenant." In the book of Revelation (and other places as well), God refers to Himself as the First and the Last, or the aleph and the tav. He truly is the strong and mighty sign that was hung on a cross. He made a covenant with us fulfilling an ancient biblical promise. The question is, will we respond back in covenant as well?

Have Enough Integrity

In Deuteronomy 32:15, God called His people *Yeshurun*, which is a tender and loving endearment. The Hebrew root meaning of *Yeshurun* is "to be upright, to have integrity." This endearment is used in the context of when Israel was forsaking her God.

Along with the Hebrew word for God, *El* makes up the word *Israel* and means "the prince of God." It seems that even though God knew that His people would rebel and chase after their own lust, by worshiping other gods, He still called them by this endearment. When talking about all who are grafted into God's family through their individual faith, whether Jew or Gentile, He consistently refers to them as *Israel*.

This is how He sees His people. Even though we sometimes fall He wants us to have the integrity to get ourselves up off the ground, ask for forgiveness, turn from our old ways, and fight the good fight.

Different Titles, Different Times

Again and again, God uses different titles for Himself throughout the Bible. Each time He reveals the voice of origin from which He wishes to speak. We do the same thing today. When speaking to our children we use a different voice than when we speak to our boss or our spouse. In life we have different capacities and authorities. Mixing them up can get us into a lot of trouble.

God, when speaking to mankind, uses different voices as well. Each voice will convey a different message. Personally, this is one of the reasons we do not like the translations today and are driven to use the original Hebrew text. The individual names of God are many times not translated. From the English texts you cannot tell what voice God is using, whether it's His personal name, *YHWH*, or a different title for Himself such as *Elohim*, which means God.

Unfortunately, almost always, when the name of God, *YHWH*, is used in the text of the Bible it is interpreted into English as "Lord." This translation, of this particular word, results in depersonalizing the reference by removing God's name, which he asked to be called by, and replacing it with a title. It would be the equivalent of someone asking you to call them by their first name, but you insist on calling them "Mister."

The Blessing of Authority

The Hebrew word for bride is *kallah* and is spelled *caf/lemed/hey*. The pictographs of these letters say "behold the blessing of authority." This is exactly what the governance of the bride of Yeshua is supposed to bring forth.

This word also means "completion and perfection, to be prepared, made ready." However, kallah also means "consumption and destruction, to be destroyed, to perish, and to waste away."

What's going on here? Why these two opposing meanings?

Recall that the book of Revelation reveals that there are two brides. The first is God's bride who will rule and reign with Him. She will be made complete and perfect, ready for her Groom. On the other hand, Satan's bride is fit only for destruction. She has allied herself with the destroyer and so she will waste away, perishing along with her groom in the place of destruction.

Satan's bride, unfortunately, is composed of all the members of mankind who covenanted with Satan and didn't ally themselves with their creator.

The Only Aramaic in the Old Testament

Daniel 4 was originally written in Aramaic. In verse 16 we learn that King Nebuchadnezzar is going to be judged by God. That judgment included having his "mind" changed from that of a man to that of a beast.

The Aramaic word for *mind* can also mean "soul." If Daniel had been writing in Hebrew he would have used the typical Hebrew word for soul, which is "nephesh." The first time this word appears is in Genesis 1:24:

> Then God said, 'Let the earth bring forth living creatures after their kind: cattle and creeping things and beasts of the earth after their kind'; and it was so.

The underlying Hebrew word in the verse above, for creatures, is "nephesh." This verse teaches us that God created all kinds of living creatures that He said were the equivalent of living souls. Unfortunately, Genesis 2:7 says:

> Then the LORD God formed man of dust from the ground, and breathed into his nostrils the breath of life; and man became a living being.

The translators, in describing the creation of man, called him a "living being" for the same word, "nephesh." What the reader loses by this inconsistency in translation is that God is trying to explain the difference between living beings and non-living things. We have very much in common with the animal kingdom when it comes to the soul.

How we're different is that God formed man with his hands rather than just speaking man into being, as he did with the animals. It's a much more intimate picture, isn't it?

Now let's take the concept of nephesh one step further. Leviticus 17:11 says:

> For the life of the flesh is in the blood, and I have given it to you on the altar to make atonement for your souls; for it is the blood by reason of the life that makes atonement.

In the verse above, the underlying Hebrew word, *nephesh*, gets interpreted as "life" twice, and as "soul" once. This inconsistency can create some confusion. By understanding that the word nephesh means "soul" and "life," this verse is communicating a very interesting concept. We think that it's the blood of Yeshua, or Jesus, that was shed on the cross that pays the price for our sins. But this verse is explaining that, in actuality, it's the soul, or the nephesh, that's contained IN the blood that actually makes the atonement.

In other words, He's offering up his soul to make atonement, knowing full well that the soul also embodies His earthly life.

Why Was Translating the Handwriting So Difficult?

Many speculate on why King Belshazzar's wise men, in the book of Daniel, couldn't translate the writing on the wall, as written by the finger of God. Certainly they were well-versed in the Hebrew language and could have interpreted the message if it had been written in Hebrew, or any of the other languages that were written or spoken in the lands that were controlled by the King.

Some also speculate that the message written on Belshazzar's wall was encrypted. From ancient times, the Jewish scribes had devised two types of encryption techniques that were known only to them — *album* and *atbash*.

In a*lbum*, the first encryption technique, the second half of the Hebrew alephbet was overlaid over the first half. So, *aleph* would then become a *lamed* and *kaf* would become a *tav*. This encryption technique was used in Isaiah 7.

In *atbash*, the second encryption technique, the second half of the Hebrew alephbet would again be overlaid over the first half, but this time *backwards*. So, the *aleph* would then be a *tav* and the *kaf* would then be a *lamed*. Jeremiah used this encryption technique in several places.

Again, this is just speculation, but the above offers one good reason why none of the other scholars were able to interpret the words written on the wall. The writing itself was "mene mene tekel peres."

The Ancient of Days

In Daniel 7:13, we see the Messiah being described as the *Ancient of Days*, which equates Him with God. But He is also being described as the *Son of Man*, which equates Him with Yeshua. This phrase, the "son of man," during the time of the life of Yeshua (or Jesus), was the most common phrase used to refer to the Messiah. It was an Aramaic phrase, pronounced "bar anash."

This phrase was not the equivalent of any son that a father might have. No Hebrew would refer to themselves or anyone else as a "son of man" in this way. This name for the Messiah evolved out of Daniel 7:13 and became the common name referring to the Messiah during the time of Yeshua 2,000 years ago.

In the New Testament we commonly see Yeshua being referred to as the *Son of Man*. This is why this statement is so profound. From our English perspective this phrase is not particularly meaningful, and certainly doesn't stand out in our minds as a designation for God, because all males are sons of men. But from a Hebrew perspective, knowing the above, you now see more clearly that the New Testament text, from the Hebrew mindset, is making a radical pronouncement. That is why the Jews of Yeshua's day were constantly accusing Him of blasphemy and sometimes picking up stones to punish Him for the same.

The Name of Our Lord, God, and Messiah

The name *Yeshua* is more profound than the translated name, *Jesus*, in our English version. "Jesus" means nothing in Hebrew. It's a construct of sounds that evolved from Hebrew, to Greek, to Latin, and then to English. For example, there is no letter in the Hebrew alphabet that makes the "j" sound. The value in knowing God's real name in Hebrew is to recognize the linkage that His real name has with other important passages we find in the Bible that make mention of that name.

Without knowing the linkage you'll never see when certain passages are making reference to the Messiah. You'll never find "Jesus" (the name) helping you in that capacity:

> "The LORD is my strength and song,
> And He has become my salvation;
> This is my God, and I will praise Him;
> My father's God, and I will extol Him. (Exodus 15:2)

This becomes more profound in helping the biblical student discover what the biblical text describes as who is actually God. The passage above states that the Lord is the strength of God's people, and He shall also be their salvation. The word there, for salvation, is the actual name of the Messiah, *Yeshua*. So the text itself reads that the Lord has become our Yeshua.

This is especially interesting when you realize that the Hebrew word translated as "Lord" is actually the intimate version of *Yahuwah*. In other words, *Yah*. This verse goes on to equate Yahuwah with Yeshua, and then equates Yeshua with *El*, or *God*. And then it equates El with *Elohim*.

On another level, "Yeshua" is spelled *yud/shen/vav/eyen/hay* in Hebrew letters. All of these letters are pictographs, and when you string together the meaning of the pictographs in Yeshua's name it communicates something unique about our Savior. And that is, "Behold the work that consumes the covenant of your eyes (or what you see)."

This links back to the fall of man. Genesis 3:5–6 tells us:

> For God knows that in the day you eat from it your eyes will be opened, and you will be like God, knowing good and evil."
> ⁶ When the woman saw that the tree was good for food, and that it was a delight to the eyes, and that the tree was desirable to make *one* wise, she took from its fruit and ate; and she gave also to her husband with her, and he ate.

The snake communicates to Eve that, upon eating the forbidden fruit and violating God's instructions, her eyes would be opened — "and you will be like God, knowing good and evil." And she saw, with her eyes, that the fruit was pleasant.

Adam and Eve, as well as all the rest of mankind

throughout the ages, have continued to make covenants with our eyes, determining for ourselves what is good. In so doing we have made a covenant with sin and death. Embedded in our Messiah's name is the work that frees us from the bondage of our sin, for His name communicates that HE will perform the work that will consume that very bondage — that attachment — that we have to the covenant of sin and death.

What "Prince" Would Have Such Authority?

In the passage below, who is this Prince of Persia who had sufficient authority to oppose God and succeeded in detaining Him? The word for prince, in verse 13 (and also in verse 20), is *sar*, which means *prince* or *archangel*. The English word *archangel* is also another word roughly equivalent to the Hebrew word for *cherub*.

> But the prince of the kingdom of Persia was withstanding me for twenty-one days; then behold, Michael, one of the chief princes, came to help me, for I had been left there with the kings of Persia. (Daniel 10:13)

As you also may be aware from reading our first book (*Lost in Translation: Rediscovering the Hebrew Roots of Our Faith*), there are three orders of angels: cherubim, seraphim, and teraphim, with the cherubim being the most powerful. They surround God's throne and serve Him constantly.

So, it appears that a fallen angel, who was once a cherub in good standing with God, was now serving Satan's kingdom and therefore tried to oppose God in the deliverance of this message to Daniel. What does that say about the importance of the message brought by the One who was detained, as found in Daniel 11 and 12? This kind of spiritual opposition to the workings of God's kingdom is not described anywhere else in the Bible when God is giving messages to his prophets. So, the message contained in the next two chapters of the book of Daniel just might be important.

Archangels are given jobs by God for His most important purposes. In Genesis 3:24, after Adam and Eve had fallen from grace, God barred the entrance to the Garden of Eden by soliciting His cherubim to stand guard with a flaming sword.

One has to wonder why God would need a cherub to guard the Garden of Eden. Couldn't just a regular old angel keep Adam and Eve from trying to get back in? Maybe God's purpose wasn't so much to prevent Adam and Eve from re-entering, but possibly to keep out the cherub who caused mankind's whole downfall in the first place: Satan.

Where Does the Word "Church" Come From?

The word "church" does not come from words in the biblical text. It is actually based on a word from ancient Babylon, via the German language. The German word for church is *kirke*, which traces its roots back to Circe, an ancient pagan god, and a Babylonian religious rite in which the pagans would stand in circles worshipping their pagan gods. We're not saying that people who use the word *church* are worshipping as pagans, but it is one of the reasons why Messianic congregations call themselves "Messianic congregations" rather than churches.

85

Where is the Garden of Eden?

Is it possible that, in the biblical text, God gives us hints about the location of the Garden of Eden? We think so.

The Garden is described as a place that was toward the East, from His location (Genesis 2:8). God has always chosen Jerusalem as the place where He would dwell, yesterday, today, and in the years to come. This is one of the reasons why we believe that, throughout the ages, virtually everybody has been fighting over the occupation of this seemingly inconsequential city in the Mideast.

In addition, Genesis tells us that a river also flowed eastward and watered the Garden. The implication is that this river flowed from the presence of God and brought life to the Garden of Eden. This is confirmed multiple places in the biblical text, one of the best known of which is in Revelation 22. That chapter describes a river, coming from the presence of God in Jerusalem, flowing eastward, where it waters, along its shore, the Tree of Life.

When mankind fell, God barred everyone from entrance to the Garden of Eden and access to the Tree of Life. His cherubim were there to protect the Garden of Eden and the Tree, and were given a flaming sword to guard the way. The word "cherubim" is the plural of "cherub." Where else do we find multiple cherubs in the Bible?

Ezekiel 1 details four of these same beings, but this time they are stationed around the throne of God. Is the Genesis text implying that the Garden of Eden, at its center, was really the location of God, His throne, and Jerusalem? Recall that the river that flowed to water the

Garden, and the river in Revelation 22 and Ezekiel 47, with the Tree of Life growing along its shores, both originate at the throne of God in Jerusalem. Also, the book of John tells us that God is the source of life, which in Hebrew, metaphorically, is represented by water. Today there is a small stream that flows from the Temple Mount, through the Kidron Valley, then eastward to the Dead Sea. What God is promising mankind is that, in His kingdom to come, that stream will once again become a river that waters the Tree of Life and thus provides food and healing to the nations.

Thus, on one level, God is representing Himself as the Tree of Life. All of this, taken together, seems to imply that the ancient garden could very well have been around or just to the east of the city of Jerusalem.

7 — End Times

Is It a Harvest or a Rapture?

The term "Rapture" is not used anywhere in the Bible. Nor does it show up in any known Christian writings before the year 1830. Neither do its basic tenets, involving two separate end-times visitations by Yeshua during which He first comes invisibly and "Raptures" His church away. As the Rapture theory proposes, He does this to allow His people to escape the Tribulation that will soon be affecting everyone else still alive on earth. The second visitation proposed in the Rapture theory is that He will come visibly to bring justice to the nations. Thus the end of the age is brought to a culmination at Armageddon.

None of this is clearly taught in scripture. It has been generated by inductive reasoning by various commentators, stringing several verses together to come to their desired conclusion. At the same time, in dealing with the absence of any mention of the Rapture as noted above, most such commentators tend to suggest that teachings about the Rapture ceased completely after the Apostolic Age, giving us more than seventeen centuries of total silence regarding what many consider one of the most important doctrines to be extrapolated from the Bible. In other words, during those seventeen centuries some of the most brilliant theologians who ever lived somehow missed it completely.

In our opinion, it makes much more sense to use the modern word "Harvest," which actually occurs in the book of Revelation, not the word "Rapture." Oh — and there are *three* harvests, by the way. These three are clearly delineated in the book of Revelation. But they occur at completely unacceptable times according to the pre-trib Rapture theory. And the group that is raptured, or "harvested" as the text says, is different than what many in the church of today preach.

These harvests can be found in Revelation 14. The first harvest is called "the taking of the Firstfruits." This is a reference to when the harvest will occur, as well as who will be harvested at that time. Firstfruits also happens to be the third of the seven festivals that God instructed His people to celebrate each year. It usually occurs in the month of April and takes place about a week after Passover.

In Revelation 14, the usage of the term "Firstfruits" is hinting at when this harvest will occur, because Firstfruits celebrated the spring barley harvest. But the biblical text also informs us that the Firstfruits are the 144,000. These are described to us in Revelation 7, and play an important role in the wedding of the lamb as groomsmen.

The second harvest in Revelation 14 is the harvest of the wheat, represented by the feast of Shavuot. Here is a wonderful description of God's Bride. The reason why most prognosticators do not identify this as the Rapture is because it's in the wrong place according to them! It happens just before the last few judgments fall on the Earth instead of occurring where they want it to occur. They want it to be at the beginning of all the tribulation found at the beginning of the book of Revelation and not in chapter 14, which describes the end of the tribulation.

There is one other harvest in Revelation 14, which is described as the "wet harvest." This occurs in the fall and includes the harvesting of all of the fruits. The fall festivals celebrate this harvest. Unfortunately, those who are identified as the wet harvest are not taken up, in contrast to the previous two, but are thrown into the winepress of God's wrath, where they suffer the final sevenfold judgments of God's wrath.

However, there is even another "rapture" or "harvest" if you will. It occurs at the end of chapter 21 and is called the Great White Throne Judgment. There the text clearly describes a resurrection of the dead, all to be judged by what they have done. But this occurs at the end of the thousand-year reign.

The Rapture Delusion

The Western church of today has been set up for a massive delusion via the widespread belief that all its members will be swept up to safety in what's commonly called the end-times "Rapture." Unfortunately, the initial Tribulation events described in the letters, seals, and trumpets in Revelation make no mention of any such Rapture.

Nonetheless, the Rapture theory teaches that God's people will not experience any of the tribulations found in Revelation. Yet nothing could be farther from the truth. In fact, God has given us a parable that predicts how people will respond to the coming of tribulation. Matthew 24:45–51 tells us the following story about a servant of God:

"Who then is the faithful and sensible slave whom his master put in charge of his household to give them their food at the proper time? "Blessed is that slave whom his master finds so doing when he comes. "Truly I say to you that he will put him in charge of all his possessions. "But if that evil slave says in his heart, 'My master is not coming for a long time,' and begins to beat his fellow slaves and eat and drink with drunkards; the master of that slave will come on a day when he does not expect him and at an hour which he does not know, and will cut him in pieces and assign him a place with the hypocrites; in that place there will be weeping and gnashing of teeth."

As end-time events unfold, this servant reacts by rejecting his Master, thinking that his Master had delayed His coming. People who are invested in a non-biblical theory that assures protection from end-times troubles could be set up to respond in the same way. As various catastrophes begin to occur, the faith of believers could also waver as they realize that Yeshua is not returning in the manner and the time frame they expected. Scripture predicts that commitment to God will grow cold among many believers (Matthew. 24:12; I Timothy 4:1). This would be especially true in an atmosphere in which belief in Messiah would not be fashionable.

Persecution, temptation, and deception have their greatest impact when faith and belief in God's Word are most weak, and especially when that Word has been misunderstood.

What Is This Nonsense About Helicopters?
Despite what many commentators have suggested over the years, the locusts that we encounter in the book of Revelation are not helicopters. Neither are they vertical

takeoff aircraft or whirling dervishes on jet-propelled pogo sticks.

In other words, the apostle John is not struggling to interpret some future technology that was nonexistent in his day. Once again we must remember that this is a Hebrew book. Without looking at everything John said from a Hebraic perspective, we'll simply never understand. He's describing what he saw, in detail, from that perspective only.

One foundational interpretive principle that so many people either disregard or simply do not know is that the key to understanding any biblical text is finding the foundation of the text and understanding that thoroughly. Any book will always come with a basis for understanding, whether it's characters or points of fact. This is also true of the Bible, and that foundation is Torah, the first five books of the Old Testament. Or, the entire Old Testament itself.

The key to understanding any principle, or metaphor, or difficult to interpret passage is to find that concept somewhere in the Bible's foundational books. This includes Revelation 9, where we see the supposed helicopters rising out of the pit. They're not helicopters at all, of course, but devils that have been locked up there.

What About Those Rings?

As we have informed people in our *Lost in Translation* series on the book of Revelation, three end-times wars will occur in the last days. It's interesting to note that the first war constitutes a group of people that mostly live contiguous to the land of Israel today. Those attackers are described in Psalm 83. Ancient names are used for the people groups in that passage, but they all end up being peoples that live immediately around Israel today. Many of them descend from Esau or Ishmael, who are known mostly as Arabs today and are brothers of the people of Israel. Most of the attackers in the first ring descended from brothers, representing the inheritance covenant.

The second End Times war will include a group of enemies that will form another ring outside of the first ring around Israel. They represent the friendship covenant and come from lands that used to be friendly with Israel. This list of allies is described in Ezekiel 38, which lie geographically just outside the ring of allies in the previous group.

The third and last war, Armageddon, constitutes a third ring. They all have had relatively little direct contact with Israel over the years, but nonetheless they have allied themselves together to destroy Israel and commandeer all her resources, both natural and developed.

Question: Will there be some sort of counter-covenant going on here, whereby Satan will rally those who will help him oppose Israel? For example, is it just coincidental that the first ring includes brothers of Israel? Is it accidental that the second ring includes groups that were once mostly friendly toward Israel?

To continue the covenant concept, the third group would include those with the most distant relationships with Israel, both now and in the ancient past.

What Does Daniel Have to Say?

Here's one of the more familiar passages from Daniel:

> 24"Seventy weeks have been decreed for your people and your holy city, to finish the transgression, to make an end of sin, to make atonement for iniquity, to bring in everlasting righteousness, to seal up vision and prophecy and to anoint the most holy place. 25So you are to know and discern that from the issuing of a decree to restore and rebuild Jerusalem until Messiah the Prince there will be seven weeks and sixty-two weeks; it will be built again, with plaza and moat, even in times of distress. 26"Then after the sixty-two weeks the Messiah will be cut off and have nothing, and the people of the prince who is to come will destroy the city and the sanctuary And its end will come with a flood; even to the end there will be war; desolations are determined. 27And he will make a firm covenant with the many for one week, but in the middle of the week he will put a stop to sacrifice and grain offering; and on the wing of abominations will come one who makes desolate, even until a complete destruction, one that is decreed, is poured out on the one who makes desolate."
> (Daniel 9:24–27)

Many prognosticators mistakenly assume that this passage from Daniel refers to the Great Tribulation, and that it lasts only seven years. However, the seven years Daniel referred to in verse 27 constitute the final seven years, which are actually just a portion of the total tribulation period prophesied in the book of Revelation. The tribulation in Revelation starts in chapter 6 and is defined all the way through chapter 19.

Meanwhile, the Ezekiel prophecy contains an especially interesting passage with respect to Magog:

> "Then those who inhabit the cities of Israel will go out and make fires with the weapons and burn them, both shields and bucklers, bows and arrows, war clubs and spears, and for seven years they will make fires of them." (Ezekiel 39:9)

This verse describes events that will occur in the immediate aftermath of the miraculous destruction of the army of Gog. For seven years the weapons of Gog will be used to fuel fires in the land of Israel. Why only seven years? Does the supply run out at the end of seven years, or is something else happening here?

We believe that the time period is seven years because only seven years are left before the coming of the King! When the Messiah comes there will be no need to make such collections in the land of Israel, for the land will be cleansed of such things when He sets up His kingdom. This confirms the text of Revelation and the understanding of the sixth trumpet representing the Magog attack on Israel, as described in Ezekiel 38 and 39.

This seven years, in which the inhabitants of Israel collect weapons and burn them, is the same seven-year time period in the book of Revelation that describes the time of the two witnesses and the False Messiah. These events are followed by the seven bowls of judgment as described in the 16th chapter of Revelation. All of these events, combined, total about seven years, and culminate in Armageddon.

A Special Blessing for Mankind?
Some people believe that God was giving to mankind a special blessing in Genesis 1:28:

> God blessed them; and God said to them, "Be fruitful and multiply, and fill the earth, and subdue it; and rule over the fish of the sea and over the birds of the sky and over every living thing that moves on the earth."

They believe that by blessing Adam and Eve God was literally both establishing and endorsing mankind's ability to dominate, control, and help usher righteousness back into the world. Even today, thousands of years later, the same folks believe that mankind is slowly restoring goodness back to the earth through that same God-given blessing.

They see the improvements in technology that enable us to enjoy longer life spans, coupled with other scientific, political, and social advancements, as fulfillments of this blessing. They also believe that, as this process continues, they will be able to help God restore His creation by finally expunging most of the imperfections caused by sin. This will then allow for the completion of God's work, which is to restore the union between God and man.

This, of course, is not our own position, and as we have stated in other books, not God's position either. In Genesis 1:28, the Hebrew word for "be" (as in "be fruitful") is *para*. The primary meaning for this word is "to bear," as in a burden. Thus Adam and Eve were given a goal to be fruitful, to fill the earth, and to subdue it. Through the righteous management of something God created and owned, mankind was to bless the earth.

And yes, it is true that the verse says that God blessed man. However, the Hebrew word translated as "bless" also conveys meanings that do not come through in English. It means "to bend the knee" (to honor someone by bowing down), "to invoke someone," "to celebrate and/or to adore."

In other words, God was modeling for Adam how to manage His creation. He was saying to Adam that "I want you to manage my estate though humility and respect. In so doing, fill the earth and subdue it."

The rabbis believe that this is the first commandment given to mankind. In accordance with the divine wish, the world is to be inhabited. And, one who neglects this has abrogated a positive commandment and will incur great punishment, because he thereby demonstrates that he does not wish to comply with the divine will to populate the world.

Yes, God does give us burdens, which have been given to us to carry. And no burden from God is too difficult for He is a kind and caring God who knows exactly what our limits are.

Satan attempted to deter God from His goal, represented by the wound on the heel, but in the process received a deadly head wound. God will step forward and destroy Satan and his plans right at the exact point when the Adversary thinks he has finally arrived at the pinnacle of his power. What a great fall this will be, for him as well as his followers.

The Lawless One — the Antichrist

> Then that lawless one will be revealed whom the Lord will slay with the breath of His mouth and bring to an end by the appearance of His coming. (2 Thessalonians 2:8)

The Greek word for lawless, in the passage above, is

anomos. In Greek, words preceded by an "a" add the idea of "no," or "law<u>less</u>." So, the remaining Greek word, *nomos*, happens to be the word that the ancient translators of the Septuagint used to translate Torah into Greek. What the word lawless in the New Testament refers to here is that the Beast, or the antichrist, will be someone who completely disregards Torah, or the English word that is used to translate Torah, "law."

It's confusing when one believes that there could be anything that Jesus has in common with the antichrist. The church of today believes that, when Jesus came, He abolished "the law." But here, in our passage, Paul is denigrating the antichrist for doing exactly the same. However, if the law had been abolished, as many Christians of today believe, why is another messiah going to come in the future to do exactly the same thing? How is that ever going to act as a sign? Wouldn't the church just say, "We already knew that!"

We believe that there is a huge contrast between these two "messiahs." The *real* one came and promoted the law. The false one will come and is described as the lawless one, for the very purpose of being able to single him out. Without knowing the laws of God, people will not be able to differentiate and contrast the two. That's why this is a sign.

In Conclusion . . .

Preparing a publication of this type provides a unique challenge to the authors. The goal may be diversity, but too much of a good thing can lead the reader down too many different paths and destroy any sense of continuity. Thus it requires of the authors a unique sense of balance for which there are no absolute guidelines.

At the same time, for the reader it requires a willingness to explore a number of subjects that may "hang loosely together," united by a common thread. In this publication, that "common thread" is the Bible itself, with special emphasis on how understanding its authors and its original language can amplify its meaning to believers from many different backgrounds.

Thus the seven subjects, as identified in the Introduction, all explore a slightly different aspect of God's message to all of us, as included in His Word. It is our hope that the information we've included may inspire our readers to do even more research on their own, to understand the Great God of the Universe to an ever-increasing extent.

He truly is our All-in-All, on many different levels at once! May the contents of this book — short and concise as it may be — help you see that same picture in an ever-brighter light.

Other Books at lostintranslation.org

Lost in Translation: Rediscovering the Hebrew Roots of our Faith *(Volume 1)*
John Klein and Adam Spears

Despite the sensational nature of its subject, *Lost in Translation: Rediscovering the Hebrew Roots of our Faith*
is written in simple, clear, rational language that relies 100 percent on the Bible as the ultimate authority.

The authors shed light on centuries of confusion surrounding subjects that are seldom addressed in modern sermons and Bible studies.

Using ancient Hebrew language and culture, the authors clarify many of the Bible's so-called "mysteries" and help the reader uncover the treasure of foundational truths that have been "lost in translation." Topics include:

• Who is the Bride of Messiah?
• Is there a difference between covenant and testa ment?
• How does the rainbow reflect God's plan for mankind?
• What is the difference between devils, demons, and nephilim?

Join us on an exciting adventure to rediscover the treasures still buried within the pages of The Book that reveal the pathway to the heart of God.

Lost in Translation: The Book of Revelation Through Hebrew Eyes *(Volume 2)*
John Klein and Adam Spears

The Book of Revelation through Hebrew Eyes is the second in the Lost in Translation three-volume series. The title says it all! This book takes a look at the first half of the book of Revelation from its Hebraic cultural and linguistic perspective. The truth of many misunderstood verses will be revealed when the light of ancient Hebrew interpretation is shone on the Bible's premiere book of end-times prophecy.

Many intriguing questions will be answered, such as:

• Who are the 144,000?
• Are all believers the Bride of Messiah?
• What are the locusts that come from the abyss?

If you're interested in this volume, we highly recommend reading the first volume, because it lays the foundation for understanding the book of Revelation.

Lost in Translation: The Book of Revelation: Two Brides — Two Destinies *(Volume 3)*
John Klein and Adam Spears

In the final volume of this series the authors explore the second half of Revelation from the perspective of a Hebrew God speaking through a Hebrew believer to an audience that was intimately familiar with the Hebrew language, culture, customs, and concepts that form both the literal and metaphorical foundation for vast portions of Revelation. In the process they answer a multitude of important questions, including:

• Whose bride are you? Can you change sides or are you stuck forever in a relationship you really don't want?
• Who or what is the False Messiah? The False Prophet?
• What is the Second Death?
• Could these catastrophes happen in my lifetime?

It is especially important for the current generation to understand the Bible's premiere book on end-times prophecy because deception will be rampant.

Anatomy of the Heavens, God's Message in the Stars
John Klein

The constellations in our night sky have captivated almost everyone throughout history and have a remarkable story to tell. It's God's most dramatic message, and it's literally written in the stars. Each of the 12 constellations plays its part in telling the overarching plan God has had since the beginning of creation.

Although Satan has used astrology to pervert God's purpose for the stars, God has provided the starry hosts to fulfill the reason for their creation. The stars were originally created for signs (Genesis 1:14) — signs that link to biblical prophecy.

Each of the 12 tribes is represented and embellished by one of the constellations. Amazingly, the position of the stars during the biblical festivals also gives insight into God's grand plan.

Family Sabbath Seder
Jodi Klein

The Family Sabbath Seder makes it easy for your family to join together in marking the beginning and closing of Sabbath, setting it off as the best day of the week. The Seder contains well-thought-out gems that have been developed by people over the centuries to aid in keeping the fourth commandment. Candle lighting, wine, bread, and havdalah blessings are in easy-to-read Hebrew transliterations so your family can correctly pronounce the Hebrew if you decide to use the Hebrew blessings.

Our tried-and-true favorite hallah bread recipes are included (with one for bread machines!) along with a question and answer page, geared to pointing out that everything you do in welcoming the Sabbath is imbued with meaning.

The Family Sabbath Seder makes it easy to establish rich traditions that will continue for generations.

Couple's Sabbath Seder
Jodi Klein

This Seder is a tool for couples to use in welcoming the Sabbath. Included are candle lighting, wine, bread, and havdalah blessings in easy-to-read Hebrew transliterations and our favorite hallah bread recipes.

The Seder will fulfill any couple's desire to please God by marking the opening and closing of the Sabbath in this special way.

Single's Sabbath Seder
Jodi Klein

Begin your Sabbath by reflecting on God with these time-honored traditions adapted specifically for the single person. You're invited to meet with Him as His special day arrives, and a tradition of using the Sabbath Seder can enrich that intimate weekly appointment.

Hanukkah Covenant Seder
Jodi Klein

This family-friendly Seder takes you through the eight nights of Hanukkah by beginning with a Hebrew blessing centering on Yeshua and transliterated phonetically so that even those unfamiliar with Hebrew can read it accurately.

This Seder is unique in that it uses color to teach about covenant and to answer the question, "How do I draw near to God?" Each night includes sections on covenant, relevant scriptures, enrichment, and the history of Hanukkah, enabling kids and adults to understand covenant and what it means to have a relationship with the Light of the World. This 60-page booklet is chock full of suggestions to make your Hanukkah more meaningful than ever.

S'firat HaOmer: Counting the Omer
Jodi Klein

Leviticus 23:15, 16 instructs us to count the omer. How do we do that? This book makes it simple, with one page for each day of the count. The short blessing and the count are in Hebrew and English, with easy-to-pronounce phonetic Hebrew. Counting the Omer is 100% user-friendly - if you can read English, you can correctly pronounce the Hebrew transliteration!

We have not seen another book that makes it so easy for you to fulfill the Leviticus 23: 15, 16 command, and you'll end up learning some Hebrew while you're at it.

Why did God instruct us to count up seven weeks to Shavuot beginning on the festival of Firstfruits? Because the wheat harvest, Shavuot, is the best harvest and represents the Groom's harvest of the Bride. There's going to be a wedding! Shavuot (Pentecost in Greek) represents the Hebrew custom of the snatching of the Bride prior to the wedding.

Counting the Omer is the intense anticipation God built into this particular holiday by requiring us to count the days leading up to it.

The Key to Your Weather Forecast
John Klein

Today, talk of the current weather forecast is one of the most common but least understood topics. This book will cut through all the confusion and allow anyone to make an accurate weather forecast. Used in a remote outdoor location or just around town, this field guide will enable you to quickly acquire an understanding of what causes the dramatic weather changes, which we all talk about, and make your own exciting predictions.

This key has been designed to make weather forecasting

fun and easy and distinguishes this book from every other on the subject. Without the need for prior instruction or aid, you can determine the weather by answering the simple questions in the key.

The promise: this book will enable you to accurately forecast the weather for the next few days in about 5 minutes.

Made in the USA
San Bernardino, CA
18 September 2015